Legacy Of Human Rights

Ehsan Sheroy

Spectra Enterprise

Legacy Of Human Rights

CONTENTS

INDEX

Chapter 1

Introduction

The tradition of common freedoms is a significant story woven into the texture of mankind's set of experiences, rising above time and boundaries to arise as a foundation of our shared mindset. As we explore the perplexing embroidery of our past, present, and future, the idea of common freedoms remains as a directing light — a demonstration of the persevering through battle for poise, balance, and equity.

At its center, the tradition of common liberties is a many-sided mosaic of wins and hardships, a narrative of mankind's determined quest for an additional equitable and caring world. Established in the acknowledgment of the inborn worth and equity, everything being equal, paying little heed to race, orientation, religion, or economic wellbeing, the excursion toward widespread basic liberties has been both laborious and rousing.

The groundworks of the advanced common freedoms development can be followed back to the outcome of The Second Great War. The detestations of the Holocaust and the extraordinary size of human experiencing incited the global local area to consider profoundly the requirement for a bunch of generally acknowledged standards to defend the intrinsic respect of each and every individual. The outcome was the Widespread Announcement of Common freedoms (UDHR), embraced by the Unified Countries General Gathering in 1948.

The UDHR, frequently hailed as an achievement in the development of basic liberties, verbalizes a dream of a reality where people are liberated from separation, viciousness, and persecution. Its 30 articles include an extensive variety of common, political, financial, social, and social privileges, shaping the bedrock of resulting basic liberties deals and shows.

However, the excursion toward understanding the goals set out in the UDHR has been not even close to straight. The tradition of common liberties is set apart by both advancement and difficulties, as countries wrestle with the perplexing errand of making an interpretation of elevated standards into unmistakable, groundbreaking activity. Over the entire course of time, different developments — social liberties, ladies' privileges, LGBTQ+ freedoms, native privileges, and that's only the tip of the iceberg — have enlightened the way ahead, testing dug in frameworks of imbalance and requesting the satisfaction of common freedoms for all.

Inborn in the tradition of basic freedoms is the acknowledgment that these standards are not static; they are dynamic, advancing because of the changing shapes of our worldwide scene. The battle for basic freedoms is continuous, adjusting to new difficulties and bridling the force of aggregate promotion to face arising dangers. From the battle against politically-sanctioned racial segregation to contemporary fights for web opportunity and ecological equity, the tradition of basic freedoms is molded by the versatility of the individuals who will not acknowledge the norm.

The worldwide talk on common liberties has extended past the domain of global discretion to pervade the day to day routines of people across the globe. Basic liberties have turned into an energizing sob for those minimized and persecuted, giving a language through which the weak can verbalize their complaints and request equity. Grassroots developments and common society associations assume a significant part in enhancing the voices of the disappointed, considering states and foundations responsible for their activities.

Chasing basic freedoms, instruction arises as a powerful device for strengthening. Mindfulness and comprehension of basic freedoms standards act as an impetus for social change, encouraging a culture of regard, resistance, and sympathy. Schools, colleges, and instructive foundations become pots for the spread of common freedoms values, supporting an age that isn't just mindful of its privileges yet additionally dedicated to maintaining the freedoms of others.

The tradition of basic freedoms is interlaced with the idea of responsibility. As countries focus on maintaining common liberties through global arrangements and shows, the significance of responsibility instruments couldn't possibly be more significant. Courts, councils, and worldwide bodies assume a crucial part in settling basic liberties infringement, guaranteeing that culprits are considered responsible for their activities. The Worldwide Lawbreaker Court (ICC) remains as a demonstration of the aggregate obligation to equity on a worldwide scale, looking to end exemption for the most deplorable violations.

Be that as it may, the quest for responsibility isn't without challenges. Sway concerns, international contemplations, and the impediments of worldwide regulation frequently confound endeavors to consider strong entertainers responsible. The tradition of basic liberties is set apart by occurrences where the journey for equity converges with the intricacies of political real factors, highlighting the requirement for proceeded with support and change.

The interconnection of basic liberties is a critical component of its inheritance. Perceiving that people frequently face converging types of segregation, the common liberties system develops to address the exceptional difficulties experienced by various gatherings. Orientation based viciousness, racial separation, and foundational monetary disparities are interconnected issues that request comprehensive, multifaceted methodologies. The tradition of common liberties requires a promise to destroying crossing types of mistreatment and making comprehensive, impartial social orders.

As innovation reshapes the shapes of our interconnected world, the tradition of basic liberties stretches out into the advanced domain. The right to protection, opportunity of articulation, and admittance to data are basic parts of the computerized privileges scene. Network safety dangers, online restriction, and the effect of computerized reasoning on human independence present new difficulties that request creative arrangements established in common freedoms standards.

Natural equity is a fundamental feature of the tradition of common freedoms in the 21st hundred years. The speeding up speed of environmental change, natural corruption, and the inconsistent dispersion of ecological weights lopsidedly influence minimized networks. The right to a solid climate is progressively perceived as principal to the more extensive basic liberties plan, stressing the interconnectedness of environmental supportability and human prosperity.

Despite worldwide difficulties, for example, the Coronavirus pandemic, the tradition of basic liberties is tried again. The pandemic uncovered and compounds prior disparities, featuring the requirement for a rights-based way to deal with general well-being. Admittance to medical care, assurance of weak populaces, and the right to precise data become vital worries, stressing the getting through pertinence of common freedoms in the midst of emergency.

The tradition of basic liberties additionally reaches out to the domain of compassionate activity. In the midst of contention and emergency, the global local area is called upon to maintain the standards of mankind, unprejudiced nature, and impartiality. Helpful associations work enthusiastically to reduce enduring, safeguard regular folks, and maintain the privileges of those impacted by struggle and catastrophic events. The convergence of basic liberties and compassionate activity highlights the basic of guaranteeing that the most defenseless are not abandoned.

The job of state run administrations in forming the tradition of common freedoms is critical. States are compelled by a sense of honor to regard, secure, and satisfy the basic liberties of their residents, with administration designs and strategies intended to protect the prosperity of all. The idea of the common agreement, wherein residents share authority with their legislatures in return for assurance and the satisfaction of freedoms, highlights the complementary connection between the state and its kin.

Transnational companies and the business area likewise assume a huge part in molding the tradition of common liberties. As strong financial entertainers, partnerships have the obligation to regard common liberties in their tasks and supply chains. The business and basic liberties system stresses the requirement for corporate responsibility, straightforwardness, and an expected level of effort to forestall and address denials of basic freedoms related with business exercises.

All in all, the tradition of basic liberties is a demonstration of the getting through journey for equity, nobility, and fairness that characterizes our common humankind. From the drafting of the Widespread Statement of Basic freedoms in the outcome of The Second Great War to the perplexing difficulties of the 21st hundred years, the excursion toward acknowledging common liberties is set apart by progress, misfortunes, and the unstoppable soul of the people who won't acknowledge treachery.

As we think about the tradition of basic liberties, we should perceive that the work is nowhere near total. The battles of the past illuminate our present, encouraging us to face the treacheries of today with the very assurance that filled the developments of days of old. The tradition of basic freedoms calls upon every age to be stewards of equity, advocates for the voiceless, and draftsmen of an existence where the innate pride of each and every individual isn't simply an ideal however a resided reality.

1.1 Brief overview of the concept of human rights

The idea of common freedoms is a primary and developing structure that expresses the innate pride and worth of each and every person, framing the reason for a fair and evenhanded worldwide society. Established in the affirmation of the general idea of human nobility, basic liberties encapsulate a bunch of standards and values that rise above social, political, and topographical limits. This concise outline investigates the verifiable development, key standards, and contemporary difficulties of the idea of basic liberties.

Authentic Development

The verifiable underlying foundations of common liberties can be followed through an embroidery of philosophical, strict, and social customs that have long perceived the crucial worth of people. Old developments, from the Code of Hammurabi to the lessons of Confucius, laid the preparation for rules that reverberation through the halls of time — thoughts that people have specific basic privileges essentially by goodness of being human.

Be that as it may, the formalization and codification of common freedoms picked up speed in the fallout of the barbarities of The Second Great War. The revulsions of the Holocaust and the far reaching acknowledgment of the requirement for an aggregate reaction to forestall such monstrosities later on prompted the drafting of the General Statement of Basic freedoms (UDHR) by the Unified Countries. Embraced in 1948, the UDHR was a pivotal record that broadcasted a typical norm for the security of major basic liberties and opportunities.

Key Standards

Comprehensiveness

At the center of the idea of basic liberties is the standard of all inclusiveness. Basic liberties are viewed as intrinsic to all people, independent of their identity, nationality, orientation, religion, or some other trademark. This all inclusiveness infers that basic freedoms are not dependent upon social or political settings but rather are essential privileges that apply to each individual by ethicalness of their humankind.

Inherent nature

Common freedoms are in many cases depicted as basic, meaning they can't be given up, moved, or removed. Despite conditions, legislatures, or cultural standards, people hold their essential common freedoms. This rule highlights that specific privileges, like the right to life, independence from torment, and opportunity of thought, inner voice, and religion, are non-debatable and characteristic for human life.

Inseparability

Basic liberties are indissoluble, interrelated, and related. The acknowledgment that common and political freedoms are interwoven with monetary, social, and social privileges shapes a foundation of the basic liberties structure. The unbreakable quality guideline stresses that the full acknowledgment of human potential requires the synchronous insurance of a range of freedoms, including the right to instruction, wellbeing, and a sufficient way of life.

Fairness and Non-Segregation

Fairness lies at the core of common liberties, and the standard of non-separation affirms that all people are equivalent under the steady gaze of the law and are qualified for equivalent insurance of their freedoms. Segregation in light of race, variety, sex, language, religion, political or other assessment, public or social beginning, property, birth, or other status is explicitly denied. This standard disallows prejudicial regulations as well as requires the end of oppressive practices and mentalities at all degrees of society.

Responsibility and Law and order

The idea of basic freedoms is unpredictably connected to law and order and responsibility. State run administrations and foundations are liable for maintaining and safeguarding common freedoms. This involves making lawful structures, laying out establishments, and guaranteeing successful solutions for basic freedoms infringement. Law and order is a crucial precondition for the security of common liberties, giving a structure inside which equity can be controlled fair-mindedly.

Global Common freedoms Instruments

Soon after the reception of the UDHR, an exhaustive structure of global deals, shows, and arrangements has been laid out to operationalize and safeguard common freedoms. These instruments cover an expansive range of freedoms, including common and political privileges, financial, social, and social freedoms, and the privileges of explicit gatherings like ladies, kids, and native people groups.

Worldwide Pledge on Common and Political Freedoms (ICCPR)

Embraced in 1966, the ICCPR is a key global deal that spotlights on common and political freedoms. It confirms privileges like the right to life, opportunity of articulation, opportunity of gathering, and the right to a fair preliminary. States gatherings to the ICCPR focus on regarding and guaranteeing the freedoms revered in the pledge, and the deal lays out systems for individual and aggregate grievances.

Global Pledge on Monetary, Social and Social Freedoms (ICESCR)

Likewise took on in 1966, the ICESCR supplements the ICCPR by underscoring monetary, social, and social freedoms. It perceives the option to work, the right to training, the right to a satisfactory way of life, and the right to wellbeing. States gatherings to the ICESCR focus on doing whatever it may take to dynamically understand these freedoms, taking into account the assets available to them.

Show on the Disposal of All Types of Victimization Ladies (CEDAW)

Embraced in 1979, CEDAW is a milestone global settlement tending to orientation based separation. It requires the disposal of victimization ladies in all circles, including lawful, political, financial, and social regions. CEDAW addresses a huge move toward perceiving and tending to the particular difficulties looked by ladies in understanding their common liberties.

Show on the Freedoms of the Kid (CRC)

Embraced in 1989, the CRC is an exhaustive settlement devoted to the security and advancement of the privileges of youngsters. It envelops common, political, monetary, social, and social privileges for kids and sets principles for their prosperity, advancement, and security from double-dealing and misuse.

Global Show on the Disposal of All Types of Racial Separation (ICERD)

Taken on in 1965, ICERD is a settlement centered around battling racial segregation. It censures racial isolation and politically-sanctioned racial segregation and requires the disposal of racial separation in the entirety of its structures. States parties focus on going to lengths to forestall, forbid, and destroy racial separation and advance comprehension and resistance among various racial and ethnic gatherings.

Show Against Torment and Other Savage, Cruel, or Debasing Treatment or Discipline (Feline)

Embraced in 1984, Feline is a settlement explicitly tending to torment and other savage, barbaric, or debasing treatment or discipline. It characterizes and disallows torment, requires states gatherings to forestall torment inside their locale, and lays out systems for the examination and indictment of those liable for torment.

Worldwide Contract on Common and Political Privileges (ICCPR) and Global Agreement on Monetary, Social and Social Freedoms (ICESCR)

These two contracts, by and large alluded to as the Worldwide Bill of Basic freedoms alongside the UDHR, put forward a complete system for the insurance and advancement of common liberties. They highlight the relationship and unification of common and political privileges with monetary, social, and social freedoms.

Contemporary Difficulties

While critical headway has been made in the acknowledgment and assurance of common freedoms, the idea faces contemporary difficulties that require continuous consideration and support.

Disintegration of City Space

In different regions of the planet, there is a developing pattern of contracting city space, with legislatures forcing limitations on opportunity of articulation, gathering, and affiliation. Columnists, activists, and common society associations frequently face provocation, control, and viciousness, subverting the fundamental job they play in advancing and safeguarding basic freedoms.

Rising Imbalance

Monetary disparity stays a tireless test, with an unbalanced grouping of riches and assets in the possession of a couple. This imbalance subverts the standards of civil rights as well as hampers the acknowledgment of monetary, social, and social privileges for enormous portions of the populace.

Outcast and Transient Privileges

The predicament of outcasts and travelers features the requirement for an extensive and privileges based way to deal with movement. Separation, xenophobia, and insufficient insurance instruments present huge difficulties to the common freedoms of those effectively dislodged from their homes.

Ecological Equity

The effect of environmental change and ecological corruption represents a danger to the satisfaction in common freedoms, especially by weak networks. The right to a sound climate and the acknowledgment of the interconnectedness between ecological manageability and basic freedoms call for creative answers for address the worldwide natural emergency.

Innovation and Basic liberties

Headways in innovation achieve new difficulties and potential open doors for basic liberties. Issues connected with computerized security, reconnaissance, online control, and the effect of man-made consciousness on human independence require cautious thought to guarantee that mechanical advancement lines up with common freedoms standards.

Worldwide Wellbeing Difficulties

Occasions like the Coronavirus pandemic highlight the interconnectedness of worldwide wellbeing and basic liberties. Guaranteeing admittance to medical care, safeguarding weak populaces, and maintaining the right to exact data become basic parts of a rights-based way to deal with general wellbeing.

1.2 Historical context: evolution of human rights over time

The development of basic liberties after some time is a mind boggling story profoundly entwined with the recurring pattern of history, mirroring the aggregate yearnings and battles of mankind to lay out a system that defends the intrinsic nobility and worth of each and every person. From the philosophical thoughts of antiquated civic establishments to the codification of standards in present day worldwide regulation, the verifiable setting of the development of basic liberties gives essential bits of knowledge into the continuous mission for equity, uniformity, and principal opportunities.

Antiquated Establishments

The underlying foundations of basic freedoms can be followed back to the old developments of Mesopotamia, Egypt, India, China, and Greece. While the idea of basic liberties as we comprehend it today was not unequivocally expressed, these early social orders laid the basis for essential rules that perceived the intrinsic worth of people.

Code of Hammurabi

In old Mesopotamia, the Code of Hammurabi (around 1754 BCE) is perhaps of the earliest known lawful code. While fundamentally worried about keeping social control and directing monetary exercises, it included arrangements that recognized the idea of equity and reasonableness, accentuating the possibility of proportionate discipline for violations.

Confucianism in Antiquated China

Confucianism, a powerful way of thinking in old China, highlighted the significance of moral excellencies, social congruity, and the prosperity of people inside a local area. Albeit not expressly outlining freedoms from a cutting edge perspective, Confucian standards featured the moral treatment of people and the obligations of rulers toward their subjects.

Greek Way of thinking

In old Greece, masterminds like Socrates, Plato, and Aristotle added to the philosophical talk on equity, morals, and the idea of humankind. While their conversations didn't straightforwardly form an idea of basic freedoms, they laid the foundation for the later improvement of moral rules that perceived the significance of individual independence and the quest for a highminded life.

Judeo-Christian Practices

The Judeo-Christian practices likewise assumed a huge part in forming the moral and moral establishments that would later impact the idea of basic freedoms. The Judeo-Christian confidence in the intrinsic worth of every individual as made in the picture of God added to the advancing comprehension of human nobility.

Magna Carta

The Magna Carta, endorsed in 1215, is a significant record throughout the entire existence of common freedoms. While it was at first a political understanding between Lord John of Britain and his nobles, it laid the basis for the rule that the ruler, as well, was dependent upon the law. This thought of law and order would later turn into a central part of basic liberties.

Illumination and Present day Political Idea

The Edification, a time of scholarly mature in the seventeenth and eighteenth hundreds of years, denoted a turning point in the development of basic liberties. Edification scholars tested customary power and supported reason, individual privileges, and the quest for joy.

John Locke

John Locke, a persuasive Edification savant, explained the idea of normal freedoms. In his "Two Compositions of Government" (1689), Locke placed that people had inborn privileges to life, freedom, and property. This thought laid the basis for the later advancement of the right to individual flexibility and confidential property.

Jean-Jacques Rousseau

Rousseau's "The Common agreement" (1762) further added to the developing talk on the freedoms of people inside a general public. He contended for the foundation of a common agreement wherein people would energetically surrender a portion of their opportunities in return for the security of their excess privileges by an all in all picked government.

Statement of the Freedoms of Man and of the Resident

The Edification standards tracked down articulation in the Statement of the Privileges of Man and of the Resident, a critical report of the French Transformation took on in 1789. This progressive announcement affirmed the balance of residents under the watchful eye of the law, the right to freedom, property, security, and protection from persecution. It turned into an essential message in the improvement of current common liberties.

Nullification of Servitude and the Introduction of Philanthropy

The nineteenth century saw critical steps in perceiving and tending to net infringement of basic freedoms, most prominently the cancelation of servitude and the development of compassionate developments.

Cancelation of Subjugation

The abolitionist development, energized by moral and strict convictions, tried to end the transoceanic slave exchange and the organization of subjection. The English Domain passed the Bondage Cancelation Act in 1833, and different countries stuck to this same pattern, denoting a urgent step towards perceiving the widespread right to opportunity.

Red Cross Development

The Red Cross, established by Henri Dunant in 1863, denoted the start of current helpful endeavors. The development planned to give help to those impacted by equipped struggles, regardless of their ethnicity, and established the groundwork for the later improvement of global philanthropic regulation.

Universal Conflicts and the General Announcement of Basic freedoms

The barbarities of The Second Great War, including the Holocaust and other mass outrages, stirred the global local area to lay out a thorough structure for the insurance of basic liberties.

Nuremberg Preliminaries

The Nuremberg Preliminaries, held after The Second Great War, denoted whenever people first were considered responsible for atrocities, violations against mankind, and decimation. The preliminaries laid out the rule that people could be considered criminally answerable for activities that abused fundamental basic freedoms.

Widespread Statement of Common liberties (UDHR)

In the outcome of The Second Great War, the Unified Countries took on the Widespread Statement of Common freedoms in 1948. Drafted under the initiative of previous First Woman of the US Eleanor Roosevelt, the UDHR was a milestone report that broadcasted a typical norm of privileges to be generally secured. It includes common, political, monetary, social, and social privileges, setting a moral and lawful starting point for the resulting improvement of basic freedoms instruments.

Cold Conflict and the Development of Basic liberties Instruments

The Virus War period, described by international strains between the US and the Soviet Association, saw both the development of common liberties standards and their instrumentalization for political purposes.

Global Agreement on Common and Political Freedoms (ICCPR) and Worldwide Contract on Financial, Social and Social Privileges (ICESCR)

Taken on in 1966, the ICCPR and the ICESCR are twin agreements that further explained on the privileges illustrated in the UDHR. They became instrumental in operationalizing basic freedoms by outlining explicit commitments and making components for oversight and requirement.

Helsinki Accords

The Helsinki Accords of 1975, endorsed by the US, the Soviet Association, and other European countries, tended to common liberties inside the setting of safety and participation. The agreements included responsibilities to regard common liberties and principal opportunities, denoting a significant stage in connecting basic freedoms to worldwide relations.

Common freedoms in the Post-Cold Conflict Time

The finish of the Virus War saw an expanded spotlight on basic liberties as a worldwide plan, with new difficulties and valuable open doors arising in a quickly changing international scene.

Show on the Privileges of the Youngster (CRC)

Embraced in 1989, the CRC addressed a milestone in perceiving the particular freedoms of youngsters. It accentuated the wellbeing of the youngster, the right to endurance and advancement, and insurance from double-dealing and misuse.

Global Crook Court (ICC)

Laid out in 2002, the ICC addresses a significant stage in the battle against exemption for the most serious global wrongdoings, including massacre, violations against humankind, and atrocities. The court gives a setting to the indictment of people liable for such violations when public purviews can't or reluctant to do as such.

Contemporary Difficulties and the Fate of Basic liberties

While huge headway has been made in the worldwide acknowledgment and assurance of common liberties, the 21st century presents new difficulties that request progressing consideration and imaginative reactions.

Arising Advancements

Headways in innovation, including man-made consciousness, biotechnology, and observation devices, present novel difficulties to basic liberties. Issues like advanced security, opportunity of articulation in the web-based space, and the moral utilization of innovation require cautious thought to guarantee that mechanical advancement lines up with common freedoms standards.

Environmental Change and Natural Equity

The speeding up speed of environmental change represents a danger to the pleasure in basic liberties, especially by weak networks. The right to a solid climate and the acknowledgment of the interconnectedness between natural manageability and basic liberties call for incorporated answers for address the worldwide ecological emergency.

Worldwide Wellbeing Difficulties

Occasions like the Coronavirus pandemic highlight the interconnectedness of worldwide wellbeing and common liberties. Guaranteeing admittance to medical services, safeguarding weak populaces, and maintaining the right to precise data become basic parts of a rights-based way to deal with general wellbeing.

Relocation and Outcast Privileges

The predicament of outcasts and travelers features the requirement for a far reaching and privileges based way to deal with relocation. Separation, xenophobia, and insufficient insurance components present critical difficulties to the common liberties of those effectively dislodged from their homes.

1.3 Importance of preserving and understanding the legacy of human rights

The significance of saving and understanding the tradition of common liberties is central in cultivating a fair, evenhanded, and merciful worldwide society. The tradition of basic liberties epitomizes the aggregate insight, battles, and accomplishments of humankind chasing general poise, equity, and equity. As we dive into the meaning of saving and appreciating this inheritance, we unwind the primary rules that support basic freedoms and the groundbreaking effect they have on people, social orders, and the world overall.

Shielding Human Pride

At the core of the tradition of basic freedoms is the major rule of protecting human respect. The acknowledgment that each individual has intrinsic worth and is qualified for essential freedoms by uprightness of being human is a foundation of the common liberties structure. Protecting this heritage is fundamental in maintaining that nobody ought to be exposed to debasing treatment, segregation, or abuse.

Understanding the tradition of basic liberties guarantees that the innate poise of every individual remaining parts a core value notwithstanding developing difficulties. It fills in as a steady update that, paying little mind to social, political, or monetary contrasts, all people share a typical humankind that merits regard and security.

Encouraging Correspondence and Incorporation

Saving and understanding the tradition of common liberties adds to the continuous battle for correspondence and incorporation. The authentic excursion of common freedoms is set apart by developments that tested prejudicial practices in view of race, orientation, religion, and different attributes. The tradition of these battles fills in as a reference point for progressing endeavors to destroy foundational imbalances and advance comprehensive social orders.

By grasping the tradition of basic freedoms, people and networks gain experiences into the significance of annihilating separation and advancing equivalent open doors for all. The battle against racial shamefulness, orientation imbalance, and different types of separation is secured in the standards laid out by common freedoms, and saving this heritage supports the obligation to building social orders where variety is praised, and each individual has the potential chance to flourish.

Maintaining Opportunity and Independence

The tradition of basic liberties support the standards of opportunity and independence, perceiving the innate right of people to go with decisions about their lives, convictions, and characters. Saving this inheritance shields the opportunity of thought, articulation, and affiliation, fundamental parts of vote based social orders where people can take part effectively and add to social, political, and social talk.

Understanding the authentic battles for opportunity and independence builds up the significance of safeguarding these freedoms despite difficulties like control, dictatorship, and limitations on individual freedoms. The tradition of basic liberties urges social orders to oppose the disintegration of opportunities and to advocate for conditions where people can practice their freedoms unafraid of response.

Cultivating Civil rights and Fortitude

Protecting and understanding the tradition of common freedoms is indivisible from the quest for civil rights and fortitude. The standards cherished in basic liberties instruments advocate for impartial admittance to assets, open doors, and fundamental administrations. The tradition of civil rights developments, including those tending to neediness, disparity, and work privileges, frames a necessary piece of the more extensive common freedoms account.

By valuing this heritage, people and social orders are propelled to take part in aggregate endeavors to address fundamental shameful acts. It builds up the thought that the prosperity of one is interconnected with the prosperity of all, advancing a feeling of worldwide fortitude. Figuring out the battles against monetary imbalance, segregation, and double-dealing highlights the basic of making social orders where equity isn't just a legitimate idea yet a resided reality.

Giving a System to Responsibility

The tradition of common liberties gives a basic system to holding people, establishments, and states responsible for their activities. Safeguarding this inheritance guarantees that the individuals who execute denials of basic liberties can be considered dependable under both public and worldwide regulation. The foundation of worldwide criminal councils and courts embodies the obligation to responsibility for the most incredibly grievous infringement.

Figuring out the verifiable setting of responsibility systems, like the Nuremberg Preliminaries after The Second Great War or the foundation of the Global Crook Court, builds up the rule that exemption for denials of basic freedoms is unsatisfactory. It fills in as an obstacle and an update that people in, influential places should be liable for their activities, adding to the development of a culture where equity beats exemption.

Supporting a Culture of Common freedoms Instruction

Protecting and understanding the tradition of common freedoms is firmly connected to the advancement of basic liberties instruction. Instruction is an incredible asset for bringing issues to light, cultivating compassion, and imparting a feeling of obligation toward the insurance of basic liberties.

By integrating the verifiable setting of common freedoms into instructive educational programs, social orders can develop a culture that values basic liberties as a common legacy.

Basic freedoms instruction goes past only communicating data; it outfits people with the decisive reasoning abilities to investigate contemporary issues through a common liberties focal point. Understanding the tradition of basic liberties gives a verifiable setting to instructors to contextualize illustrations on resilience, variety, and the significance of dynamic municipal commitment.

Protecting Against Relapse

The tradition of common liberties fills in as a defense against relapse into tyranny, mistreatment, and the disintegration of vote based values. History is packed with occasions where the freedoms of people were stomped all over by severe systems, prompting broad affliction and unfairness. Safeguarding the tradition of basic freedoms is essential for forestalling the repeat of such dim periods in mankind's set of experiences.

By grasping the battles against despotism, control, and dictator rule, social orders can invigorate themselves against the infringement of belief systems that look to subvert common freedoms. The inheritance fills in as an aggregate memory, helping social orders to remember the delicacy of freedoms and the requirement for steady cautiousness to safeguard them.

Exploring Contemporary Difficulties

The conservation and comprehension of the tradition of basic liberties are especially relevant in exploring the complicated difficulties of the contemporary world. Issues like the effect of innovation on protection, the worldwide evacuee emergency, and the multifacetedness of separation require nuanced reactions established in common freedoms standards.

The tradition of basic freedoms offers a compass for tending to arising difficulties. It gives a bunch of moral rules that can direct people, policymakers, and activists in tracking down arrangements that regard human pride, maintain equity, and advance equity. The standards enunciated in the tradition of basic liberties stay important and versatile, offering an immortal starting point for tending to the developing scene of common freedoms issues.

Encouraging Worldwide Coordinated effort

Protecting and understanding the tradition of common liberties encourages worldwide coordinated effort in tending to shared difficulties. Common liberties are intrinsically widespread, rising above borders and social contrasts. The tradition of worldwide participation, as exemplified by the development of the Unified Countries and the reception of widespread basic liberties instruments, highlights the aggregate liability of the worldwide local area.

In a world interconnected by profession, correspondence, and shared natural difficulties, safeguarding the tradition of basic freedoms is fundamental for building cooperative structures. It builds up the possibility that countries should cooperate to resolve worldwide issues, perceiving that the security of basic liberties is an aggregate undertaking that rises above international contemplations.

The tradition of basic freedoms remains as a demonstration of the getting through quest for equity, respect, and fairness that has denoted the course of mankind's set of experiences. This inheritance is definitely not a static artifact yet a powerful power, formed by the aggregate battles, wins, and developing moral cognizance of social orders across time. It envelops the central rules that declare the inborn worth of each and every person, regardless of their experience, and tries to lay out a widespread system that shields basic opportunities and human pride.

At its center, the tradition of common liberties follows its foundations to the result of The Second Great War — a period scarred by the significant monstrosities of the Holocaust and the destruction created by worldwide struggle. In light of these unmatched detestations, the global local area looked to fashion a way toward an additional fair and sympathetic world. The outcome was the Widespread Statement of Basic liberties (UDHR), embraced by the Unified Countries General Get together in 1948.

The UDHR, frequently hailed as an achievement in the development of common liberties, verbalizes a dream of a reality where people are liberated from segregation, viciousness, and persecution. Its 30 articles incorporate an extensive variety of common, political, financial, social, and social privileges, shaping the bedrock of resulting basic freedoms deals and shows. The tradition of the UDHR is implanted in its optimistic standards, mirroring a common obligation to the conviction that basic freedoms are not dependent upon identity, nationality, or some other variable however are the inheritance of each and every individual.

As the tradition of common freedoms unfurled, it became entwined with the battles of different developments for equity and equity. The social equality development in the US, drove by figures like Martin Luther Lord Jr., looked to destroy racial isolation and fundamental segregation. The women's activist development pushed for orientation uniformity and ladies' freedoms, testing settled in standards that propagated orientation based imbalances. LGBTQ+ freedoms developments battled against segregation and for the acknowledgment of the privileges of people independent of their sexual direction or orientation character.

The tradition of basic freedoms grows past the domain of formal statements and arrangements. It is carved in the aggregate memory of the people who battled for equity even with affliction. Figures like Nelson Mandela, who persevered through long periods of detainment to battle politically-sanctioned racial segregation in South Africa, and Malala Yousafzai, who opposed the

Taliban to advocate schooling for young ladies, represent the unstoppable soul that portrays the tradition of basic freedoms. Their accounts act as encouraging signs, outlining that the quest for equity can conquer apparently inconceivable deterrents.

Inborn in the tradition of common liberties is the rule of comprehensiveness. Common freedoms are not honors gave by states or establishments; they are characteristic for human life. This all inclusive nature highlights that paying little heed to social, strict, or political contrasts, certain freedoms are unavoidable and apply to all people. The tradition of comprehensiveness challenges relativism and social excellence, attesting that the essential standards of common freedoms rise above topographical lines and different conviction frameworks.

The resoluteness of common freedoms is one more basic part of the heritage. The interconnectedness of common and political freedoms with financial, social, and social privileges shapes a far reaching system for human pride. The right to life, freedom, and security is indivisible from the right to instruction, wellbeing, and a satisfactory way of life. The tradition of indissoluble nature stresses that the full acknowledgment of human potential requires the concurrent security of a range of freedoms.

Balance and non-segregation are central standards woven into the tradition of common freedoms. The battle against racial separation, orientation based viciousness, and different types of foul play highlights the basic of perceiving and destroying frameworks that sustain disparity. The inheritance provokes social orders to defy predispositions, biases, and oppressive works on, encouraging a culture where the intrinsic equity of all people isn't just recognized yet effectively maintained.

At the core of the tradition of basic freedoms lies the rule of responsibility. Legislatures, establishments, and people bear the obligation of maintaining and safeguarding common freedoms. The foundation of global councils, like the Worldwide Crook Court (ICC), connotes a pledge to considering those liable for gross infringement of basic liberties responsible for their activities. The tradition of responsibility supports that exemption for denials of basic freedoms is inconsistent with the standards of equity and law and order.

Training arises as a strong instrument in saving and communicating the tradition of common liberties. Mindfulness and comprehension of common freedoms standards act as impetuses for social change, cultivating a culture of regard, resilience, and compassion. Common freedoms instruction outfits people with the information to perceive and challenge foul play, enabling them to become advocates for the privileges of others. Schools, colleges, and instructive organizations become critical conductors for giving the qualities cherished in the tradition of basic freedoms to people in the future.

The tradition of basic liberties reaches out into the advanced domain as innovation reshapes the shapes of our interconnected world. The right to security, opportunity of articulation, and admittance to data become basic parts of the computerized privileges scene. Difficulties like web-based oversight, reconnaissance, and the moral ramifications of computerized reasoning brief a reevaluation of common freedoms with regards to quickly developing innovations. Safeguarding the heritage includes adjusting the basic freedoms structure to address new difficulties while maintaining the persevering through rules that support it.

Natural equity is an essential feature of the tradition of common freedoms in the 21st hundred years. The speeding up speed of environmental change, ecological corruption, and the inconsistent dispersion of natural weights lopsidedly influence minimized networks. The right to a sound climate, cherished in the heritage, calls for pressing activity to address the interconnected difficulties of ecological maintainability and basic freedoms. The heritage requests a pledge to feasible practices, preservation, and impartial admittance to assets to guarantee the prosperity of present and people in the future.

Saving and understanding the tradition of common liberties is certainly not a uninvolved activity however a continuous obligation to address contemporary difficulties. The heritage gives a guide to exploring the intricacies of the cutting edge world, offering rules that can direct people, states, and establishments chasing equity, equity, and nobility. As the heritage unfurls, it stays a living story, formed by the activities and decisions of every age.

Contemporary difficulties, like the worldwide evacuee emergency, general wellbeing crises, and the ascent of dictatorship, highlight the persevering through pertinence of the tradition of common freedoms. The predicament of displaced people and travelers requires a reaffirmation of the standards of non-separation and the option to look for shelter. General wellbeing emergencies, exemplified by the Coronavirus pandemic, feature the crossing point of wellbeing and common freedoms, underscoring the significance of fair admittance to medical services and exact data.

The ascent of dictatorship and the disintegration of vote based values challenge the center standards of the common freedoms heritage. As legislatures reduce opportunities, stifle disagree, and subvert law and order, the inheritance turns into a revitalizing point for those supporting for a majority rules system and basic freedoms. The battles contrary to dictator rule act as a wake up call that the tradition of basic freedoms isn't invulnerable to dangers and should be effectively shielded by those resolved to its standards.

All in all, the tradition of basic freedoms is an embroidery woven with the strings of history, battles, and yearnings for an additional equitable and empathetic world. Protecting and understanding this inheritance is an aggregate liability that rises above lines and ages. It requires an unfaltering obligation to the standards of comprehensiveness, unification, balance, and responsibility.

As the heritage keeps on unfurling in the 21st 100 years, it provokes social orders to stand up to new real factors and adjust the common liberties system to address arising difficulties. The tradition of common freedoms is a living story that calls upon people, networks, and countries to effectively participate in the continuous quest for equity, equity, and poise for all. In protecting and understanding this heritage, mankind finds an impression of its past as well as a directing light toward a future where the standards of common liberties are worshipped as well as completely acknowledged in the texture of regular daily existence.

Chapter 2

The Birth of Human Rights

The idea of basic freedoms, as we grasp it today, has profound authentic roots that stretch across societies and civilizations. While the expression "basic liberties" might be moderately later, the possibility that people have inborn freedoms by goodness of their humankind has been advancing over hundreds of years.

The starting points of common liberties can be followed back to old civic establishments where different philosophical and strict customs laid the foundation for the acknowledgment of major privileges. In antiquated India, for instance, the idea of "dharma" enveloped moral and social obligations, accentuating the significance of treating others with decency and regard. Also, antiquated Chinese way of thinking, especially Confucianism, stressed the significance of moral way of behaving and the common regard between people.

In the West, the foundations of basic liberties can be found in the lessons of traditional Greek thinkers like Socrates, Plato, and Aristotle. These scholars investigated thoughts connected with equity, uniformity, and the idea of individuals.

Aristotle's idea of regular regulation, which set that specific standards are inborn in human instinct and can be observed through reason, laid the basis for the later improvement of common freedoms.

The Judeo-Christian practice likewise assumed a huge part in molding the moral groundworks of common liberties. The Good book, with its accentuation on the respect of every person as made in the picture of God, affected Western moral idea. The possibility of the innate worth and fairness surprisingly tracked down articulation in scriptural lessons, adding to the later advancement of basic freedoms standards.

As social orders advanced, so did the enunciation and acknowledgment of individual freedoms. The Magna Carta, endorsed in 1215, is frequently thought to be a central report throughout the entire existence of basic freedoms. While its essential spotlight was on controlling the force of rulers, it set a trend by recognizing specific legitimate insurances for people and laying out the rule that even rulers were dependent upon the law.

The Renaissance and the Illumination time frames checked critical achievements in the development of common liberties. The Renaissance achieved a restored interest in humanism, underlining the worth and capability of people. The Edification, with its accentuation on reason, science, and individual independence, further high level the thought that people have inborn freedoms.

The savant John Locke, a critical figure of the Edification, explained the idea of regular privileges in the seventeenth 100 years. Locke's thoughts, especially the idea of a "common agreement" among people and government, laid the preparation for the later improvement of popularity based standards and common liberties. As per Locke, people reserve the privilege to life, freedom, and property, and state run administrations are founded to safeguard these freedoms.

The American and French Transformations of the late eighteenth century were critical crossroads throughout the entire existence of common freedoms. The US Statement of Freedom, wrote by Thomas Jefferson in 1776, proclaimed that "all men are made equivalent" and enriched with "unalienable Privileges, for example, "Life, Freedom, and the quest for Joy." This fundamental report mirrored the impact of Edification thoughts and set a trend for the consideration of common liberties standards in established records.

Essentially, the French Announcement of the Freedoms of Man and of the Resident, took on in 1789 during the French Unrest, broadcasted the inborn privileges of people and stated the balance of all residents under the watchful eye of the law. These progressive statements denoted a defining moment in the acknowledgment of basic freedoms as a focal part of administration.

The nineteenth century saw the progressive development of common freedoms standards, frequently because of social and political difficulties. The abolitionist development, which tried to end servitude, drew on the intrinsic respect and equity of all people as an ethical starting point for its goal. The battle for ladies' freedoms picked up speed, testing winning ideas of orientation disparity and pushing for equivalent treatment under the law.

The helpful development of the nineteenth 100 years, prodded by figures like Henry Dunant and the Red Cross, stressed the requirement for the security of people during seasons of equipped clash. The idea of philanthropic regulation started to come to fruition, mirroring a developing consciousness of the effect of fighting on regular citizen populaces and the requirement for worldwide guidelines to relieve human misery.

The mid twentieth century achieved critical international changes and the result of two universal conflicts. The detestations of The Second Great War, including the Holocaust and far reaching monstrosities, highlighted the pressing requirement for a worldwide obligation to basic freedoms. The global local area, through the recently shaped Joined Countries, tried to address these worries and forestall future abominations.

The Widespread Statement of Basic liberties (UDHR), embraced by the Unified Countries General Get together in 1948, remains as a milestone throughout the entire existence of common freedoms. Drafted by delegates from different social and lawful foundations, the UDHR declared a bunch of crucial privileges and opportunities to which all individuals are entitled. It confirmed the inborn pride and uniformity of every individual and set a typical norm for the security of basic liberties all over the planet.

Eleanor Roosevelt, the main impetus behind the drafting of the UDHR, assumed an essential part in its reception. As the seat of the Unified Countries Basic liberties Commission, she worked resolutely to connect contrasts among part states and guarantee the announcement's general pertinence. The UDHR's reception denoted a significant second when the worldwide local area met up to explain a common vision of basic liberties.

The resulting many years saw the advancement of global basic liberties instruments and organizations. Deals like the Worldwide Pledge on Common and Political Freedoms and the Global Agreement on Monetary, Social and Social Privileges, both embraced in 1966, further expounded on unambiguous privileges and laid out systems for their requirement. These pledges, along with the UDHR, structure the Global Bill of Common freedoms.

The foundation of the Unified Countries Common freedoms Committee in 2006 denoted a proceeded with obligation to the advancement and security of basic liberties at the worldwide level. The board, made out of part states chose by the Overall Gathering, is liable for tending to basic liberties infringement and advancing discourse on worldwide common freedoms issues.

While critical headway has been made in the worldwide field, difficulties to the acknowledgment of common liberties persevere. Issues like destitution, segregation, furnished struggle, and ecological debasement keep on influencing people all over the planet. The mission for common freedoms stays a continuous battle, requiring aggregate endeavors to address both verifiable shameful acts and arising dangers to human nobility.

The idea of common freedoms has likewise extended to envelop new boondocks in the 21st hundred years. Progressions in innovation and correspondence have brought up issues about the crossing point of common freedoms and advanced privileges. Issues like security, opportunity of articulation, and admittance to data in the advanced age have become fundamental to the talk on common liberties in an interconnected world.

The developing idea of basic liberties likewise requires a consistent assessment of social viewpoints and the all inclusiveness of freedoms. While the UDHR is outlined as a general record, various social, strict, and philosophical practices might decipher and focus on privileges in an unexpected way. Adjusting the all inclusiveness of common freedoms with deference for social variety stays a mind boggling and continuous test.

The battle for common liberties isn't bound to the domain of regulation and strategy; it is profoundly entwined with social developments and activism. From the beginning of time, people and networks have prepared to request their privileges and challenge severe frameworks. From the social liberties development in the US to the counter politically-sanctioned racial segregation battle in South Africa, grassroots developments play had a significant impact in propelling the reason for common freedoms.

The job of schooling in advancing common liberties couldn't possibly be more significant. Common freedoms training, both formal and casual, assumes a crucial part in encouraging a culture of regard for human respect and uniformity. By outfitting people with information about their limitations, instruction turns into an incredible asset for engaging networks and testing foundational treacheries.

The acknowledgment of common liberties is naturally connected to the idea of human nobility. The possibility that every individual has intrinsic worth, no matter what their experience, qualities, or conditions, is at the center of the basic freedoms system. Human nobility fills in as the ethical starting point for the security of individual privileges and the advancement of equity and uniformity.

As the world wrestles with contemporary difficulties, including worldwide pandemics, environmental change, and international strains, the significance of a vigorous common freedoms system turns out to be considerably more clear.

The Coronavirus pandemic, for example, has featured the interconnectedness of wellbeing, financial, and social privileges. Endeavors to address the pandemic's effect should be grounded in a common liberties approach that focuses on the prosperity and respect, all things considered.

The introduction of basic liberties is a continuous story, molded by verifiable occasions, philosophical reflections, lawful turns of events, and the enthusiastic endeavors of people and networks. It is an account of progress and difficulties, of wins and difficulties. The excursion towards the acknowledgment of basic freedoms is an aggregate undertaking that requires supported responsibility, discourse, and cooperate.

2.1 Exploration of the Universal Declaration of Human Rights (1948)

The Widespread Statement of Common freedoms (UDHR), embraced by the Unified Countries General Get together on December 10, 1948, remains as a memorable achievement in the continuous journey for the acknowledgment and security of central basic liberties. Conceived out of the remains of The Second Great War and the monstrosities committed during that contention, the UDHR was an aggregate reaction by the global local area to guarantee that the detestations of the conflict wouldn't be rehashed and that a typical obligation to human nobility would win.

The drafting of the UDHR was an intricate and cooperative interaction that elaborate delegates from different social, lawful, and philosophical foundations. The Commission on Common liberties, laid out by the Unified Countries in 1946, assumed a pivotal part in forming the statement. Under the initiative of previous First Woman of the US, Eleanor Roosevelt, the commission left on the aggressive errand of drafting a report that would explain the standards of basic freedoms and stand as an encouraging sign for people in the future.

The UDHR starts with a preface that establishes the vibe for the statement. It proclaims that acknowledgment of the intrinsic pride and of the equivalent and basic privileges of all individuals from the human family is the underpinning of opportunity, equity, and harmony on the planet. The prelude mirrors a guarantee to the possibility that common freedoms are not dependent upon identity, nationality, or some other trademark yet are all inclusive and material to all individuals.

Article 1 of the UDHR lays out the rule of uniformity and non-segregation, expressing that all people are conceived free and approach in poise and privileges. This primary article makes way for the ensuing articles, every one of which explains on unambiguous privileges and opportunities that are innate to all people.

The announcement is separated into two fundamental parts. The initial segment frames common and political freedoms, while the subsequent part tends to monetary, social, and social privileges. The division isn't intended to infer an order of privileges yet rather perceives the reliance and unbreakable quality of every basic freedom.

The common and political privileges illustrated in the UDHR incorporate the right to life, freedom, and security of individual (Article 3); independence from torment and debasing treatment (Article 5); the right to a fair preliminary (Article 10); and the right to opportunity of thought, heart, and religion (Article 18), among others. These privileges are intended to safeguard people from erratic state activities, guaranteeing that individuals can live liberated from persecution and appreciate fundamental opportunities.

The financial, social, and social privileges enunciated in the UDHR envelop the option to work (Article 23); the right to training (Article 26); the option to take part in social life (Article 27); and the option to partake in the advantages of logical advancement (Article 27), among others. These privileges underline the significance of making conditions that empower people to carry on with an honorable existence, liberated from neediness and hardship.

One of the central standards of the UDHR is the possibility that basic freedoms are interrelated, associated, and unified. This implies that common and political freedoms can't be completely acknowledged without additionally guaranteeing monetary, social, and social privileges, as well as the other way around. The all encompassing methodology of the UDHR perceives that human prosperity is a multi-layered idea that requires the security of an expansive scope of freedoms.

The drafting system of the UDHR involved input from delegates of various legitimate practices and social foundations, bringing about a record that draws on a rich embroidery of worldwide viewpoints. While the statement mirrors the impact of Western legitimate practices, it likewise integrates components from assorted social, strict, and philosophical customs. This inclusivity was a purposeful decision, expected to make a report that would resound with individuals from all edges of the world.

The UDHR was embraced by a mind-boggling greater part of the Unified Countries part states, with just eight abstentions. The reception of the statement denoted an earth shattering event, as it addressed an aggregate obligation to the possibility that basic liberties are all inclusive and rise above public limits. The UDHR turned into the main worldwide archive to broadcast the equivalent and unavoidable freedoms of each and every person, paying little heed to identity, nationality, orientation, or some other distinctive variable.

Eleanor Roosevelt assumed a vital part in supporting the reason for common freedoms and working with the reception of the UDHR.

As the seat of the Unified Countries Basic freedoms Commission, she explored through the difficulties of different viewpoints and contending interests to guarantee the report's all inclusiveness. Her authority and conciliatory abilities were instrumental in fashioning agreement among part states and conquering snags during the drafting system.

The UDHR's reception was a critical stage, however it was just the start of a more extensive development to cherish basic liberties in worldwide regulation. Soon after the reception of the UDHR, the Assembled Countries kept on expanding on standards by creating global arrangements and shows additionally expounded on unambiguous privileges and laid out components for their insurance.

The Worldwide Agreement on Common and Political Privileges (ICCPR) and the Global Contract on Financial, Social and Social Freedoms (ICESCR), both embraced in 1966, are key parts of what is altogether known as the Global Bill of Basic liberties. These contracts, alongside the UDHR, structure the fundamental system for the assurance and advancement of basic liberties at the global level.

The ICCPR centers around common and political privileges, including the right to life, opportunity of articulation, and the right to a fair preliminary. It lays out a structure for observing and upholding these freedoms through the Common liberties Board of trustees, a group of free specialists that surveys state reports and hears individual grumblings.

Then again, the ICESCR tends to monetary, social, and social privileges, for example, the option to work, the right to instruction, and the right to a sufficient way of life. The Board of trustees on Financial, Social and Social Freedoms, made under the ICESCR, screens the execution of these privileges by states parties.

Together, the UDHR, ICCPR, and ICESCR structure an extensive and interconnected set of worldwide common liberties norms. They give a typical establishment to the security of basic freedoms, guaranteeing that people are ensured a scope of common, political, financial, social, and social privileges.

The execution of the privileges illustrated in these worldwide instruments depends on the responsibility and activities of states parties. At the point when a state turns into involved with a common freedoms deal, it takes on the obligation to regard, safeguard, and satisfy the privileges revered in that settlement. States are expected to report occasionally on their advancement in carrying out these privileges, and global observing bodies assume a pivotal part in considering them responsible.

The all inclusive nature of basic liberties suggests the worldwide relevance of these standards as well as the common obligation of the global local area to maintain and advance them.

The Unified Countries and its different offices, alongside non-legislative associations and common society, assume key parts in pushing for basic freedoms, observing their execution, and giving a stage to discourse and collaboration.

Throughout the long term, the comprehension of basic freedoms has developed, prompting a more profound enthusiasm for the interconnection of privileges and the requirement for a more comprehensive and diverse methodology. Diversity perceives that people might encounter various types of separation in view of variables like race, orientation, sexual direction, handicap, from there, the sky is the limit. This understanding has impacted how common freedoms are both conceptualized and executed.

The UDHR's standards have additionally affected the improvement of local common liberties frameworks. Provincial associations, like the European Court of Common liberties, the Between American Court of Basic freedoms, and the African Court on Human and People groups' Privileges, have been laid out to address common liberties issues well defined for their individual areas. These territorial instruments supplement the worldwide system given by the Unified Countries and add to the requirement of basic liberties at a more restricted level.

The idea of common freedoms has extended to incorporate new aspects and difficulties that have arisen in the contemporary world. Mechanical progressions, for example, have led to conversations on computerized privileges and the need to safeguard protection, opportunity of articulation, and admittance to data in the advanced age. The fast speed of innovative change presents the two open doors and difficulties for the assurance of basic freedoms, requiring continuous variation of legitimate systems and standards.

Ecological freedoms have likewise acquired unmistakable quality as the worldwide local area wrestles with the effect of environmental change and natural corruption. The acknowledgment that a sound climate is essential to the satisfaction in common freedoms has prompted conversations on the requirement for a rights-based way to deal with ecological security.

Difficulties to the comprehensiveness of common freedoms persevere, for certain pundits contending that the idea is intrinsically Western-driven and doesn't sufficiently represent assorted social points of view. Others battle that basic freedoms talk has been instrumentalized for political purposes and specifically applied, prompting allegations of affectation and twofold principles.

The strain between widespread standards and social relativism brings up significant issues about the execution of basic liberties in assorted social orders. Finding some kind of harmony requires progressing exchange, social responsiveness, and an affirmation that the standards of basic freedoms are intended to be comprehensive and versatile to various settings.

The battle for common liberties go on universally, with various occasions of infringement and difficulties that request consideration and activity. Furnished clashes, displaced person emergencies, separation, and financial disparities stay diligent issues that test the global local area's obligation to maintaining basic freedoms.

The job of schooling in advancing basic liberties couldn't possibly be more significant. Common freedoms training fills in as a basic device for bringing issues to light, encouraging a culture of regard for human pride, and enabling people to advocate for their privileges. Endeavors to incorporate common liberties instruction into school educational plans, preparing projects, and local area drives add to building a more educated and connected with worldwide populace.

All in all, the investigation of the General Statement of Common freedoms uncovers a rich embroidery of verifiable setting, cooperative endeavors, and developing points of view on the idea of basic liberties. The statement, embraced in the fallout of The Second Great War, addresses an aggregate obligation to the possibility that each individual is qualified for central privileges and opportunities, paying little heed to identity, nationality, or some other distinctive component.

The UDHR's standards have filled in as an establishment for the improvement of worldwide basic freedoms regulation, including the Global Bill of Common liberties containing the ICCPR and ICESCR. The interconnected and reliant nature of common liberties underscores the requirement for a comprehensive methodology that tends to common, political, financial, social, and social freedoms.

While progress has been made in the worldwide acknowledgment of common freedoms, challenges persevere, and the advancing idea of the world acquaints new aspects with the talk. The obligation to basic liberties requires continuous discourse, transformation to contemporary difficulties, and an aggregate work to address the industrious infringement that undermine the pride and prosperity of people all over the planet. The investigation of the UDHR isn't simply a verifiable activity yet a continuous excursion towards an all the more, impartial, and freedoms regarding world.

2.2 Key individuals and events that influenced the development of human rights

The improvement of basic freedoms as an idea and a legitimate system has been molded by the commitments of key people and vital occasions from the beginning of time. From philosophical scholars to activists on the ground, these people play played pivotal parts in articulating, advancing, and protecting the possibility that all people have inborn freedoms by ethicalness of their mankind.

Perhaps of the earliest figure throughout the entire existence of common liberties is Cyrus the Incomparable, the pioneer behind the Persian Domain in the sixth century BCE. Cyrus is eminent for his popular Chamber, a declaration engraved on an earth chamber that is much of the time thought about one of the earliest contracts of common freedoms. In it, Cyrus proclaims that he will permit all individuals inside his domain to rehearse their own religions and customs and underlines the significance of opportunity and respect.

Pushing ahead in time, the Illumination period in the seventeenth and eighteenth hundreds of years assumed a crucial part in molding the scholarly underpinnings of basic liberties. Illumination scholars like John Locke, Jean-Jacques Rousseau, and Voltaire laid the foundation for the possibility that people have inborn freedoms that states are committed to safeguard. Locke's idea of normal privileges, Rousseau's common agreement hypothesis, and Voltaire's promotion for opportunity of articulation all added to the advancing talk on individual freedoms.

The American Transformation in the late eighteenth 100 years and the drafting of the US Constitution further high level the conceptualization of freedoms. Persuasive figures like Thomas Jefferson, one of the chief creators of the Announcement of Autonomy, and James Madison, the essential drafter of the Bill of Privileges, implanted standards of individual freedoms and securities against government oppression in these fundamental reports.

At the same time, the French Unrest, motivated by Illumination goals, denoted a defining moment in the journey for basic liberties. The Statement of the Freedoms of Man and of the Resident, embraced in 1789, attested the equivalent and basic privileges of all residents and impacted resulting announcements of common liberties around the world. The French Unrest's accentuation on freedom, correspondence, and club reverberated worldwide and added to the spread of basic liberties standards.

In the nineteenth hundred years, the abolitionist development arose as a strong power supporting for the finish of servitude. Abolitionists like Frederick Douglass, Harriet Beecher Stowe, and William Lloyd Post assumed key parts in testing the dehumanizing organization of servitude and advancing the innate respect and uniformity, all things considered, paying little heed to race.

The Seneca Falls Show in 1848 denoted a turning point throughout the entire existence of ladies' freedoms. Coordinated by activists, for example, Elizabeth Cady Stanton and Lucretia Mott, the show delivered the Statement of Opinions, which requested equivalent privileges for ladies, including the option to cast a ballot. The ladies' testimonial development that followed looked to get casting a ballot rights for ladies and added to the more extensive battle for orientation correspondence.

Henry Dunant, a Swiss finance manager and compassionate, assumed a significant part in the improvement of worldwide helpful regulation. Seeing the enduring of injured warriors on the front line at the Clash of Solferino in 1859, Dunant pushed for the foundation of willful help associations to really focus on the wiped out and injured during seasons of equipped struggle. His endeavors prompted the establishing of the Global Advisory group of the Red Cross and the reception of the Principal Geneva Show in 1864.

As the twentieth century unfolded, figures like W.E.B. Du Bois and Booker T. Washington became conspicuous voices in the social equality development in the US. Du Bois, a researcher and lobbyist, helped to establish the Public Relationship for the Headway of Minorities Individuals (NAACP) and supported for equivalent freedoms and open doors for African Americans. Washington, a teacher and counselor to presidents, stressed professional instruction and monetary independence for African Americans.

The detestations of The Second Great War and the Holocaust significantly affected the advancement of current common freedoms. The Nuremberg Preliminaries, held to indict Nazi conflict lawbreakers, laid out the rule that people could be considered responsible for perpetrating monstrosities, regardless of whether they were following up on orders from an administration. The preliminaries set a trend for considering people responsible for infringement of global regulation, adding to the foundation of the Worldwide Lawbreaker Court in the cutting edge time.

Eleanor Roosevelt, the previous First Woman of the US, arose as a focal figure in the drafting of the Widespread Statement of Common freedoms (UDHR). As the seat of the Unified Countries Common liberties Commission, she assumed a significant part in exploring the different viewpoints of part states and guaranteeing the comprehensiveness of the statement. Her conciliatory abilities and obligation to common freedoms were instrumental in the reception of the UDHR in 1948.

René Cassin, a French legal scholar and Nobel laureate, made huge commitments to the drafting of the UDHR. He assumed a key part in orchestrating the different proposition set forth by commission individuals and in forming the last text of the statement. Cassin's work on the UDHR highlighted the significance of lawful mastery and worldwide cooperation in the advancement of common liberties norms.

Mahatma Gandhi, the head of the Indian freedom development, utilized peaceful common insubordination as a useful asset for social and political change. His way of thinking of Satyagraha, signifying "truth-power" or "soul-force," roused developments for social equality and opportunity all over the planet. Gandhi's accentuation on peacefulness and equity significantly affected the improvement of basic liberties standards.

The finish of The Second Great War and the making of the Unified Countries gave a chance to lay out a worldwide obligation to basic liberties. The UDHR, took on in 1948, arose as an essential record that broadcasted the intrinsic pride and equivalent privileges of every person. The statement drew on the commitments of people from different social, strict, and legitimate foundations and set a typical norm for basic freedoms insurance.

In the US, the Social liberties Development of the 1950s and 1960s, drove by figures like Martin Luther Lord Jr., Rosa Parks, and Malcolm X, tried to end racial isolation and separation. The development accomplished critical achievements with the Social liberties Demonstration of 1964 and the Democratic Freedoms Demonstration of 1965, which planned to destroy organized prejudice and guarantee equivalent privileges for all residents.

Nelson Mandela, a vital figure in the counter politically-sanctioned racial segregation development in South Africa, turned into a global image of protection from mistreatment and a defender of compromise. Mandela's initiative was instrumental in finishing politically-sanctioned racial segregation and laying out a vote based and comprehensive South Africa. His obligation to pardoning and solidarity resounded worldwide and left an enduring heritage in the battle against treachery.

The women's activist development that picked up speed in the last 50% of the twentieth century focused on issues of orientation disparity and segregation. Activists like Betty Friedan, Gloria Steinem, and Simone de Beauvoir tested cultural standards and upheld for ladies' freedoms. The Assembled Countries announced the 1970s the Global Ladies' Ten years, prompting critical progressions in perceiving and tending to orientation based separation.

The battle for LGBTQ+ privileges likewise picked up perceivability and speed in the late twentieth hundred years. The Stall riots in 1969 denoted a urgent second in the LGBTQ+ freedoms development, prompting expanded promotion for equivalent privileges, acknowledgment, and security against segregation in view of sexual direction and orientation personality.

The finish of the Virus Battle in the late twentieth century set out open doors for the development of basic liberties standards. The fall of the Berlin Wall in 1989 and the disintegration of the Soviet Association added to a changing worldwide scene, with additional opportunities for the advancement and security of basic freedoms in previously shut social orders.

Aung San Suu Kyi, a Burmese favorable to a majority rules system pioneer and Nobel laureate, turned into an image of tranquil obstruction against harsh systems. Put detained at home for a long time, Suu Kyi's commitment to a majority rules government and common freedoms gathered global help. Her possible ascent to political unmistakable quality in Myanmar showed the persevering through force of peaceful obstruction even with tyranny.

The foundation of the Global Crook Court (ICC) in 2002 addressed a critical stage chasing equity for worldwide violations. The ICC is engaged to arraign people for destruction, violations against mankind, atrocities, and the wrongdoing of animosity. The court fills in as a system for considering culprits responsible and adding to the counteraction of future outrages.

Malala Yousafzai, a Pakistani lobbyist for female schooling and the most youthful ever Nobel Prize laureate, turned into a worldwide image of boldness notwithstanding difficulty. Getting through a death endeavor by the Taliban, Malala proceeded with her support for young ladies' schooling and ladies' privileges, rousing individuals all over the planet with her strength and assurance.

In the 21st 100 years, the convergence of common freedoms and innovation has turned into a noticeable issue. Informants like Edward Snowden uncovered government observation programs, starting discussions about the right to security in the advanced age. Activists and associations progressively center around guaranteeing that headways in innovation don't encroach on principal basic liberties.

The People of color Matter development, which acquired unmistakable quality during the 2010s, advocates for the privileges and respect of Dark people, especially with regards to police viciousness .

2.3 Examination of the post-World War II cra and the need for a global commitment to human rights

The post-The Second Great War time denoted a groundbreaking period in worldwide history, described by the phenomenal pulverization of the conflict and the acknowledgment of the requirement for an aggregate obligation to basic freedoms. The abhorrences of the conflict, including the Holocaust and far and wide barbarities, highlighted the dire need for a global system that would keep such monstrosities from happening once more. The result of The Second Great War saw the foundation of the Unified Countries and the drafting of the Widespread Statement of Common freedoms (UDHR), mirroring an aggregate assurance to fabricate a world in light of the standards of equity, fairness, and the innate nobility, everything being equal.

The obliteration created by The Second Great War was not bound to the actual annihilation of urban communities and foundation. The conflict uncovered the profundities of human savagery and the limit with respect to fundamental viciousness against whole populaces. The Holocaust, wherein 6,000,000 Jews were efficiently killed by the Nazis, uncovered the outrageous results of uncontrolled separation and the dehumanization of whole networks. The Nuremberg Preliminaries, held to arraign war crooks, featured the requirement for responsibility for people who carry out barbarities, accentuating the rule that people, no matter what their authority positions, could be considered liable for violations against mankind.

Because of the significant difficulties presented by the conflict, the global local area looked to lay out another system that would forestall such barbarities later on. The Unified Countries, established in 1945, arose as a focal foundation committed to advancing global collaboration and forestalling clashes that could prompt broad denials of basic freedoms. The preface to the UN Contract communicates the assurance to "reaffirm confidence in major common freedoms, in the respect and worth of the human individual, in the equivalent privileges of people and of countries enormous and little."

The drafting of the General Statement of Common liberties (UDHR) was a vital second in the post-The Second Great War period. The statement, embraced by the Unified Countries General Gathering in 1948, addressed a worldwide agreement on the essential privileges and opportunities to which all people are entitled. The drafting system included delegates from different social, legitimate, and philosophical foundations who tried to make a record that would reverberate generally.

Eleanor Roosevelt, the previous First Woman of the US, assumed a focal part in the drafting of the UDHR as the seat of the Unified Countries Basic freedoms Commission. Her authority, conciliatory abilities, and obligation to common freedoms were instrumental in exploring the assorted viewpoints of part states and guaranteeing the comprehensiveness of the announcement. The UDHR mirrors a blend of commitments from people, for example, René Cassin, a French legal scholar and Nobel laureate, who assumed a vital part in molding the last text of the statement.

The UDHR starts with an introduction that explains the central standards of basic liberties, stressing the intrinsic nobility and equivalent freedoms of all individuals from the human family. The prelude recognizes the examples gained from the barbarities of The Second Great War and the need to advance opportunity, equity, and harmony on the planet. It makes way for the ensuing articles, every one of which explains on unambiguous privileges and opportunities that are considered vital for the prosperity and pride of people.

The statement is a complete record that tends to common and political privileges, as well as financial, social, and social freedoms. Article 3 broadcasts the right to life, freedom, and security of individual, while Article 21 asserts the option to partake in government and the option to approach admittance to public assistance. Articles 22 and 23 perceive the right to government managed retirement, work, and a satisfactory way of life, underscoring the interconnectedness of common and political privileges with monetary, social, and social freedoms.

The UDHR's acknowledgment of monetary, social, and social freedoms was earth shattering, as it recognized that common liberties include securities against government oppression as well as the right to an honorable way of life, schooling, and social interest.

This all encompassing way to deal with common freedoms mirrored a comprehension that the prosperity of people is interconnected and can't be completely acknowledged without tending to a wide scope of privileges.

The reception of the UDHR in 1948 denoted a notable second when the worldwide local area met up to confirm a common vision of basic freedoms. The statement, despite the fact that non-restricting, set a typical norm for common liberties insurance and gave a moral and lawful starting point for ensuing worldwide deals and shows. The standards explained in the UDHR turned into the foundation of what is currently known as the Worldwide Bill of Basic freedoms, which incorporates the

UDHR, the Global Pledge on Common and Political Privileges (ICCPR), and the Worldwide Contract on Financial, Social and Social Privileges (ICESCR).

The post-The Second Great War time likewise saw the foundation of instruments for the authorization and security of basic freedoms at the global level. The Unified Countries Basic liberties Chamber, laid out in 2006, is entrusted with tending to common freedoms infringement and advancing discourse on worldwide basic freedoms issues. Particular organizations like the Workplace of the Great Chief for Basic freedoms (OHCHR) work to advance and safeguard common liberties universally and offer help to states in satisfying their common liberties commitments.

The acknowledgment of common freedoms as a worldwide concern requires a guarantee to widespread qualities that rise above public boundaries. Nonetheless, the execution of basic freedoms standards faces various difficulties, including social relativism, political obstruction, and the contending interests of states. Finding some kind of harmony between the comprehensiveness of common liberties and regard for social variety stays a continuous test that requires exchange, social responsiveness, and a promise to shared standards.

Social relativism, as an idea, sets that basic freedoms can't be general in light of the fact that various societies might have particular qualities and standards. Pundits contend that the inconvenience of Western-driven common freedoms guidelines might ignore the variety of social points of view and sabotage the standards of self-assurance. Notwithstanding, defenders of widespread common freedoms contend that specific essential standards, like the preclusion of torment or segregation, ought to be appropriate all around, rising above social varieties.

Political protection from the execution of basic liberties can appear in different structures, going from dictator systems stifling difference to strong states subverting worldwide components for common freedoms authorization. The guideline of state power, while a central part of worldwide relations, can be summoned to safeguard legislatures from responsibility for denials of basic liberties. Adjusting regard for state power with the basic to shield people from manhandles requires cautious tact and worldwide collaboration.

The contending interests of states, frequently determined by financial and international contemplations, can prevent the viable implementation of common liberties principles. States might focus on public interests over worldwide commitments, prompting circumstances where monetary and political coalitions outweigh basic freedoms contemplations. Tending to this challenge requires a nuanced approach that urges states to perceive the drawn out advantages of maintaining basic liberties for strength, improvement, and worldwide collaboration.

The battle for basic freedoms reaches out past lawful systems and worldwide foundations to grassroots developments and common society activism. Since the beginning of time, people and networks have assembled to request their freedoms and challenge harsh frameworks. The social liberties development in the US, drove by figures like

Martin Luther Ruler Jr., Rosa Parks, and Malcolm X, fills in as a strong illustration of how grassroots activism can achieve extraordinary change.

In the 21st hundred years, the coming of innovation has both worked with basic freedoms support and introduced new difficulties. The computerized age has focused on the convergence of basic liberties and innovation, with issues like web-based security, opportunity of articulation, and admittance to data becoming the overwhelming focus. Informants like Edward Snowden have uncovered government reconnaissance programs, starting discussions about the harmony between public safety and individual security.

Ecological privileges have acquired unmistakable quality as the worldwide local area wrestles with the effect of environmental change and natural debasement. The acknowledgment that a solid climate is vital to the pleasure in common liberties has prompted conversations on the requirement for a rights-based way to deal with natural security. The relationship of basic freedoms and the climate highlights the significance of addressing ecological difficulties to guarantee the prosperity of present and people in the future.

The post-The Second Great War period has seen critical headways in the acknowledgment and security of explicit gatherings' freedoms. The ladies' freedoms development, the LGBTQ+ privileges development, and the inability privileges development have all added to growing the comprehension of basic liberties to incorporate the privileges of generally minimized and mistreated gatherings. The battle for orientation equity, acknowledgment of different sexual directions and orientation characters, and backing for the freedoms of people with inabilities reflect continuous endeavors to address multifaceted types of separation.

Chapter 3

Foundational Principles

Central standards support the actual pith of our reality, giving a steady structure whereupon social orders, establishments, and people construct how they might interpret the world. These standards act as the bedrock of our aggregate qualities, molding the course of mankind's set of experiences and impacting the direction of civilizations. Looking at these fundamental standards uncovers the complicated trap of thoughts, convictions, and methods of reasoning that have woven themselves into the texture of human progress, rising above time and social limits.

At the center of these standards lies the idea of human pride, an inborn worth that perceives the innate worth and uniformity, everything being equal. This crucial rule shapes the foundation of moral and moral structures across different social orders, asking mankind to approach each other with deference and sympathy. The thought of human nobility stretches out past social and geological limits, filling in as a widespread standard that rises above contrasts and joins individuals in their common mankind.

Lined up with the rule of human nobility is the idea of equity, a persevering through good that tries to lay out reasonableness, value, and the assurance of individual privileges. Equity, as a basic guideline, appears in different structures, going from general sets of laws that expect to maintain law and order to social developments upholding for equivalent open doors and admittance to assets. The quest for equity mirrors mankind's aggregate goal to make an existence where every individual is managed the cost of the chance to flourish, unburdened by segregation or persecution.

Implanted inside the basic standards is the acknowledgment of the significance of opportunity and independence. Human social orders have long wrestled with the pressure between individual freedom and the requirement for aggregate request. Finding some kind of harmony, these standards recognize the privileges of people to articulate their thoughts, decide, and seek after their desires while likewise perceiving the need of shared liability and cultural union.

Fundamental to the comprehension of primary standards is the guideline of correspondence, which endeavors to kill separation in light of race, orientation, religion, or other erratic variables. The quest for correspondence includes destroying fundamental hindrances and moving instilled biases to make a more comprehensive and just society. By perceiving and redressing verifiable treacheries, social orders try to produce a way towards genuine uniformity, where each individual has the potential chance to flourish no matter what their experience.

In the domain of administration, the guideline of a majority rules system stands tall as a directing reference point for social orders trying to guarantee the cooperation and portrayal of their residents. A majority rule government, in its different structures, enables people to have a voice in the choices that shape their lives. Established in the possibility of self-administration, this essential guideline mirrors the conviction that the authenticity of power emerges from the assent of the represented, encouraging a feeling of shared liability and responsibility.

Instruction, as a basic guideline, arises as a groundbreaking power that enables people and social orders. The quest for information and scholarly development fills in as an impetus for progress, development, and social turn of events. Schooling not just outfits people with the abilities and information expected to explore the intricacies of the world yet in addition cultivates decisive reasoning and a more profound comprehension of one's place in the public eye.

The guideline of supportability takes on expanding significance despite worldwide difficulties, for example, environmental change and natural debasement. Perceiving the limited idea of assets, social orders are constrained to take on rehearses that guarantee the prosperity of current and people in the future. Manageability, as a basic standard, prompts a reconsideration of human exercises and their effect in the world, empowering the improvement of capable and naturally cognizant practices.

Moral contemplations, entwined with essential standards, guide people and social orders in exploring complex moral scenes. The investigation of morals digs into inquiries of good and bad, ideals and bad habit, molding the ethical compass that guides human way of behaving. Whether established in strict convictions, philosophical tenets, or social practices, moral standards give a system to people to pursue choices that line up with their qualities and add to everyone's benefit.

Entwined with the texture of basic standards is the guideline of sympathy, underscoring the significance of compassion and figuring out in human connections. Empathy rises above individual contrasts and advances a feeling of interconnectedness, empowering individuals to stretch out graciousness and backing to each other. In the midst of difficulty, the rule of sympathy fills in as a binding together power, cultivating strength and fortitude inside networks.

The standard of correspondence, frequently communicated in the adage "do unto others as you would have them do unto you," highlights the significance of common regard and collaboration. This primary rule recognizes the association of people and social orders, featuring the possibility that activities have results that resound through the complicated embroidered artwork of human connections. Correspondence empowers a feeling of obligation towards others and advances the prosperity of the system.

In the domain of innovation and development, the standard of moral direct becomes the dominant focal point, encouraging people and associations to think about the more extensive effect of their manifestations on society. As innovation keeps on progressing at a remarkable speed, moral contemplations become significant in guaranteeing that logical advancement lines up with the prosperity of mankind. Moral standards in innovation envelop issues like protection, security, and the mindful advancement of man-made consciousness, directing the mix of development into the structure holding the system together.

The standard of social variety praises the wealth of human encounters, perceiving the worth of alternate points of view, customs, and lifestyles. Social variety isn't only an unmistakable element of the human experience however a core value that advances inclusivity, understanding, and the protection of social legacy. Embracing variety cultivates a worldwide local area that blossoms with the trading of thoughts and the festival of the bunch manners by which humankind communicates itself thoughts.

Even with difficulty and struggle, the standard of harmony arises as a directing light, upholding for discretionary arrangements and the goal of questions through exchange. Harmony, as a central rule, challenges the damaging powers of war and brutality, empowering social orders to look for choices that focus on participation and compromise. The quest for harmony includes tending to underlying drivers of contention, encouraging grasping between assorted networks, and advancing worldwide joint effort.

Wellbeing and prosperity, as central standards, highlight the significance of guaranteeing admittance to quality medical care and elevating all encompassing ways to deal with physical and mental health. Perceiving wellbeing as an essential basic liberty, social orders endeavor to make frameworks that focus on preventive measures, fair admittance to clinical assets, and the disposal of variations in medical services results. The guideline of wellbeing reaches out past individual prosperity, incorporating the more extensive objective of making networks that twist and flourish.

The guideline of civil rights urges social orders to stand up to imbalance and work towards making a fair and comprehensive world. Civil rights tends to foundational hindrances that sustain separation, upholding for strategies and drives that make everything fair and enable minimized networks. As a basic standard, civil rights prompts a reconsideration of force elements and the reallocation of assets to guarantee that all people have the chance to lead satisfying lives.

The standard of monetary equity interlaces with civil rights, stressing the requirement for fair dispersion of assets and open doors. Financial equity challenges frameworks that propagate neediness, double-dealing, and inconsistent admittance to abundance. As an essential standard, monetary equity calls for strategies that advance impartial financial turn of events, address pay disparity, and set out open doors for people to accomplish monetary prosperity.

In the domain of worldwide relations, the standard of tact guides connections between countries, advancing discourse and collaboration as choices to struggle. Tact, as a fundamental standard, perceives the interconnectedness of the worldwide local area and the significance of cultivating positive relations between countries. It fills in as a system for settling questions, tending to shared difficulties, and advancing common figuring out on the world stage.

Chasing information and progress, the standard of logical request assumes an essential part, uplifting interest, investigation, and the deliberate journey for understanding. Logical request, as a primary rule, rises above social and geological limits, giving an all inclusive structure to propelling information. It includes thorough philosophies, peer survey, and a guarantee to confirm based thinking, molding the manner in which humankind fathoms the regular world.

The guideline of individual independence stresses the right of people to go with decisions about their own lives, liberated from excessive outer impact. Individual independence, as a central standard, meets with thoughts of individual flexibility and self-assurance. It requires the acknowledgment of assorted life ways and the security of people's freedoms to pursue choices that line up with their qualities and yearnings.

Chasing after truth, the standard of scholarly uprightness highlights the significance of genuineness, straightforwardness, and the quest for information without predisposition.

Scholarly trustworthiness, as a basic standard, guides scholastic and insightful undertakings, elevating a promise to truth-chasing and the dispersal of exact data. It fills in as a defend against falsehood and the twisting of realities, maintaining the trustworthiness of scholarly pursuits.

The rule of common freedoms remains as a demonstration of the widespread privileges that shield the nobility and prosperity of people. Basic liberties, as central standards, incorporate an expansive scope of common, political, financial, social, and social freedoms. They act as a moral and legitimate structure, testing rehearses that disregard the innate worth of people and supporting for the security of human nobility on a worldwide scale.

The standard of ecological stewardship highlights the obligation of people and social orders to really focus in the world and protect its biological systems. Ecological stewardship, as a primary standard, perceives the interconnectedness of human exercises and the regular world. It calls for manageable practices, protection endeavors, and an aggregate obligation to shielding the climate for people in the future.

Genuinely trustworthy in the domain of morals, the standard aides people in keeping a feeling of moral completeness and consistency in their activities. Uprightness, as a primary standard, includes adjusting one's way of behaving to moral qualities, even notwithstanding difficulties or enticements. It fills in as a foundation for trust, responsibility, and the upkeep of moral principles in private and expert undertakings.

The guideline of intergenerational obligation calls upon current ages to think about the effect of their activities on people in the future. Intergenerational obligation, as a basic standard, urges social orders to take on feasible practices, protect social legacy, and address issues, for example, environmental change with a drawn out point of view. It mirrors a familiarity with the interconnectedness of time and the requirement for moral dynamic that rises above prompt satisfaction.

Chasing imagination and development, the standard of opportunity of articulation assumes a significant part, cultivating a climate where different thoughts and viewpoints can prosper. Opportunity of articulation, as an essential standard, safeguards the right of people to voice their viewpoints, participate in imaginative articulation, and add to public talk. It fills in as a shield against oversight and adds to the energy of scholarly and social life.

The guideline of local area fortitude underlines the significance of aggregate activity and shared help notwithstanding difficulties. Local area fortitude, as a central rule, ties people together in a common obligation to the prosperity of the local area. It includes cooperation, compassion, and an acknowledgment of the strength that emerges from bound together endeavors to address shared objectives and concerns.

In the domain of morals, the guideline of obligation prompts people to think about the results of their activities and take responsibility for their effect on others and the world. Obligation, as a primary standard, stretches out to individual, social, and natural settings, encouraging people to go with moral decisions that add to everyone's benefit. It includes a feeling of obligation and an acknowledgment of the interconnectedness of individual activities inside bigger frameworks.

The guideline of social lowliness guides people in moving toward different societies with a receptive outlook, regard, and an eagerness to learn. Social lowliness, as a central standard, provokes generalizations and urges people to draw in with social contrasts without assumption or judgment. It includes a nonstop course of self-reflection and a pledge to understanding and esteeming the extravagance of different social viewpoints.

Chasing cultural prosperity, the rule of social union highlights the significance of encouraging solid securities and a feeling of having a place inside networks. Social union, as a basic guideline, includes addressing factors that add to social division and pursuing establishing comprehensive conditions where people feel associated and upheld. It perceives the job of social connections in advancing psychological wellness, versatility, and generally speaking cultural wellbeing.

The guideline of strength recognizes the limit of people and networks to adjust, recuperate, and flourish notwithstanding misfortune. Versatility, as a primary rule, includes building the abilities, assets, and emotionally supportive networks expected to explore difficulties and return from mishaps. It mirrors the comprehension that affliction is an intrinsic piece of the human experience and highlights the significance of encouraging strength at individual and cultural levels.

Chasing truth and information, the guideline of scholarly interest urges people to address, investigate, and look for a more profound comprehension of the world. Scholarly interest, as a primary guideline, drives logical request, scholastic pursuits, and the imaginative investigation of thoughts. It includes an eagerness to challenge presumptions, participate in deep rooted learning, and embrace the delight of revelation.

The guideline of inclusivity advances the production of conditions where people of all foundations, capacities, and characters feel esteemed and included. Inclusivity, as a fundamental standard, challenges separation and predispositions, cultivating a feeling of having a place for everybody inside a local area or society. It includes deliberate endeavors to destroy obstructions and make spaces where variety isn't just endured yet celebrated.

The guideline of sympathy welcomes people to comprehend and discuss the thoughts of others, cultivating empathy and association. Compassion, as a central rule, fills in as a scaffold across contrasts, advancing comprehension and shared help.

It includes undivided attention, viewpoint taking, and a veritable worry for the prosperity of others. In cultural settings, sympathy adds to the improvement of arrangements and practices that focus on the requirements of assorted networks.

The standard of flexibility perceives the unique idea of the world and urges people and social orders to embrace change and development. Flexibility, as an essential rule, includes an eagerness to learn, develop, and develop because of moving conditions. It mirrors a comprehension that adaptability and receptiveness to groundbreaking thoughts are fundamental for exploring the intricacies of a quickly influencing world.

The standard of lowliness urges people to move toward existence with a feeling of humility, perceiving the impediments of information and understanding. Lowliness, as a fundamental standard, includes a readiness to gain from others, recognize missteps, and embrace a deep rooted excursion of personal development. It counters self-importance and cultivates a receptive way to deal with the different points of view and encounters of others.

Chasing significant lives, the guideline of direction underlines the significance of characterizing one's qualities and goals. Reason, as an essential rule, includes adjusting one's activities to a feeling of importance and adding to an option that could be more significant than oneself. It gives a compass to exploring life's decisions and difficulties, directing people towards a feeling of satisfaction and fulfillment.

The guideline of interconnectivity perceives the unpredictable trap of connections that tight spot people, social orders, and the normal world. Interconnectivity, as a fundamental standard, prompts an all encompassing comprehension of the results of activities on different levels. It includes perceiving the reliance of natural, social, and monetary frameworks and settling on decisions that add to the prosperity of the whole interconnected trap of life.

Genuinely trustworthy chasing moral direct, the rule guides people to maintain a feeling of moral completeness and consistency in their activities. Respectability, as a fundamental guideline, includes adjusting conduct to moral qualities and keeping up with trustworthiness, in any event, when confronted with difficulties or enticements. It fills in as a foundation for trust, responsibility, and the conservation of moral guidelines in private and expert undertakings.

3.1 In-depth analysis of the core principles underlying human rights

Basic liberties, an idea imbued in the texture of contemporary society, fills in as a foundation of moral and legitimate structures across the globe. Established in the acknowledgment of innate poise and worth, these privileges seek to protect the prosperity of each and every person, rising above limits of identity, nationality, and ideology. To set out on an inside and out investigation of the center standards hidden common freedoms, it is basic to dive into the authentic development, philosophical establishments, and the legitimate contraption that supports this essential structure.

The starting points of basic liberties can be followed back to antiquated developments, where simple thoughts of equity and decency arose. In any case, the conventional explanation of common freedoms acquired noticeable quality in the fallout of The Second Great War, a period set apart by remarkable monstrosities and a worldwide obligation to forestall the repeat of such repulsions. The Widespread Statement of Basic freedoms (UDHR), took on by the Unified Countries General Gathering in 1948, remains as a milestone record that explains the key standards of common liberties. Created in the outcome of the Holocaust and the destruction fashioned by the conflict, the UDHR mirrors an aggregate assurance to lay out a general norm for the security of human poise.

At the core of common liberties lies the rule of human poise — an inborn and natural quality that each individual has by ethicalness of being human. This primary idea highlights that regardless of societal position, orientation, race, or some other trademark, every individual is qualified for a degree of regard and thought. Poise fills in as the wellspring from which different freedoms stream, stressing the natural worth of each and every person and shaping the bedrock whereupon the structure of basic liberties is raised.

Thoughtfully, basic liberties draw motivation from different moral customs, going from regular regulation hypotheses to deontological and utilitarian points of view. Regular regulation places that specific freedoms are innate in human instinct and can be observed through reason and moral reflection. Defenders of this point of view contend that moral standards are not dependent upon human regulations or social standards but rather are established in an otherworldly moral request. Interestingly, deontological hypotheses, prominently expressed by Immanuel Kant, declare that specific activities are intrinsically correct or off-base, regardless of their outcomes. Kant's clear cut basic, which orders regarding people as closures in themselves, lines up with the common freedoms system, underscoring the characteristic worth of every individual.

Besides, utilitarian viewpoints add to the moral underpinnings of basic freedoms by zeroing in on the advancement of generally speaking prosperity and bliss. While utilitarianism generally stresses the best really great for the best number, the common liberties system tempers this point of view by focusing on the security of individual privileges even notwithstanding likely aggregate advantages. These philosophical establishments all in all illuminate the regulating premise regarding common liberties, giving a strong moral structure that rises above social and philosophical contrasts.

A urgent part of basic liberties is the comprehensiveness of their application. The rule of comprehensiveness affirms that basic liberties are not dependent upon social relativism or dependent upon the impulses of individual countries. All things being equal, they are viewed as inborn to all people by excellence of their mankind. This obligation to comprehensiveness is revered in the UDHR, which broadcasts that "all people are conceived free and rise to in nobility and privileges."

The comprehensiveness of basic liberties fills in as a countermeasure against social relativism, testing the idea that works on disregarding common liberties can be legitimate on social grounds.

While the idea of all inclusiveness frames the bedrock of common freedoms, its application isn't without challenges. Pundits contend that the burden of Western-driven values in the pretense of widespread common freedoms might be socially imperialistic. They battle that different social, strict, and philosophical viewpoints ought to be viewed as in the plan and use of basic freedoms norms. Finding some kind of harmony among comprehensiveness and social responsiveness stays a continuous test in the worldwide talk on common liberties.

Connected unpredictably to the standard of all inclusiveness is the thought of indissoluble nature. Basic freedoms are frequently ordered into common, political, financial, social, and social privileges. The standard of unbreakable quality declares that these privileges are reliant and commonly building up, framing an interconnected web that supports the general prosperity of people and networks. For example, the right to instruction (a social and social right) is firmly connected to one side to opportunity of articulation (a common and political right). The acknowledgment of the indissoluble nature of freedoms highlights the requirement for an extensive and incorporated way to deal with basic liberties, forestalling the particular prioritization of specific privileges to the detriment of others.

Equity and non-segregation address center rules that cut across different basic freedoms instruments. The standard of equity attests that all people are qualified for similar thought and security of their privileges, without separation based on race, orientation, religion, or some other trademark. Non-segregation, a conclusion to balance, denies crooked qualifications and commands the equivalent satisfaction in freedoms for all. These standards reverberate in global lawful instruments like the Show on the

End of All Types of Victimization Ladies (CEDAW) and the Show on the Freedoms of the Youngster (CRC), the two of which highlight the basic of guaranteeing equivalent privileges for all, regardless old enough, orientation, or some other variable.

The rule of correspondence likewise converges with the idea of value, which perceives that equivalent treatment may not necessarily lead to impartial results. In specific circumstances, governmental policy regarding minorities in society and designated measures are crucial for address authentic treacheries and fundamental disparities. Value recognizes that the beginning stage for people and networks might contrast, requiring customized mediations to guarantee that the advantages of basic freedoms are open to all.

Interest and consideration are vital to the powerful acknowledgment of basic freedoms. The option to take part in dynamic cycles that influence one's life is cherished in different common freedoms instruments. This rule highlights the significance of comprehensive administration structures that permit different voices to be heard.

Comprehensive cooperation upgrades the authenticity of direction as well as adds to the ID of setting explicit arrangements that address the interesting necessities of various networks.

Straightforwardness and responsibility are critical in maintaining common liberties. The straightforwardness of government activities, combined with components for responsibility, guarantees that people with great influence are considered answerable for their activities. Admittance to data is a central part of straightforwardness, engaging people to be educated members in the public eye. Responsibility components, including lawful cycles and global councils, assume a urgent part in tending to basic freedoms infringement and preventing future offenses.

The idea of human security grows the customary comprehension of safety past the domain of state-driven worries to include the prosperity of people. Human security stresses the insurance of people from a wide exhibit of dangers, including monetary hardship, ecological debasement, and wellbeing emergencies. This all encompassing methodology lines up with the sweeping idea of common liberties, recognizing that security isn't exclusively a component of state power yet is inherently connected to the insurance and satisfaction of individual privileges.

Social relativism represents a critical test to the comprehensiveness of common liberties. Pundits contend that social, strict, and verifiable settings shape the translation and execution of basic freedoms, requiring a nuanced approach that obliges different viewpoints. While the comprehensiveness of basic liberties stays a primary guideline, a comprehensive and socially delicate exchange is fundamental for overcome any barrier between all inclusive principles and nearby real factors.

The guideline of human nobility, as the north star of basic freedoms, incorporates the intrinsic worth of every person. This inborn worth orders the acknowledgment and assurance of the independence, organization, and innate worth of each and every person. Human nobility fills in as both the beginning stage and the objective of the common liberties venture, directing the plan of privileges and the assessment of their effect on people and networks.

The idea of human pride is firmly connected to independence, the capacity of people to settle on conclusions about their own lives. Independence is a focal principle of common liberties, appearing morally justified to opportunity of thought, heart, and religion, as well as the right to protection. The security of independence recognizes that people are the best adjudicators of their own advantages and yearnings, and basic freedoms act as a safeguard against unjustifiable obstruction in private decisions.

Basic liberties likewise perceive the guideline of non-retrogression, which sets that once a specific degree of freedoms insurance is achieved, it ought not be switched. This rule prepares for backward strategies that subvert recently accomplished freedoms and guarantees a consistent direction towards the improvement of basic liberties norms.

Non-retrogression is especially significant in the midst of financial starkness or political movements, where the impulse to disintegrate privileges for the sake of practicality might emerge.

The nexus between common freedoms and a majority rules system is significant. A vote based system isn't simply a type of administration however a framework that maintains and builds up common liberties standards. The option to take part in the administration of one's nation, as revered in the Global Contract on Common and Political Freedoms (ICCPR), is a foundation of popularity based social orders. Popularity based administration gives the institutional system to the security of common liberties, with balanced governance, law and order, and regard for principal opportunities comprising fundamental components of a lively vote based system.

Common and political privileges, like opportunity of articulation, affiliation, and gathering, are vital to the working of vote based social orders. These privileges enable people to participate out in the open talk, express contradiction, and consider people with great influence responsible. The right to a fair and unprejudiced preliminary, one more key common and political right, shields people against inconsistent state activity and guarantees law and order.

Financial, social, and social freedoms supplement common and political privileges, shaping the establishment for a fair and impartial society. The option to work, the right to schooling, and the right to a satisfactory way of life are fundamental parts of monetary, social, and social privileges. The acknowledgment of these privileges isn't just an ethical goal yet additionally adds to the general prosperity and steadiness of social orders.

The strengthening of defenseless and minimized bunches is a focal precept of basic liberties. Ladies' freedoms, native privileges, and the privileges of minorities are vital elements of the basic liberties system. Orientation fairness, as expressed in CEDAW, perceives that victimization ladies isn't just an infringement of basic freedoms yet in addition an obstruction to social and monetary advancement. Native privileges underscore the conservation of social personality and the security of hereditary grounds, recognizing the verifiable shameful acts incurred upon native networks.

Kids' privileges, as cherished in the CRC, perceive the one of a kind weaknesses of youngsters and highlight their qualification to unique security and care. The Show on the Privileges of People with Inabilities (CRPD) supports the rule of incorporation, accentuating that people with incapacities ought to partake in similar freedoms as their non-debilitated partners. The basic liberties system's accentuation on inclusivity reaches out to all people, regardless of their experience, guaranteeing that the advantages of privileges are available to the whole range of human variety.

The developing idea of basic liberties is exemplified by the acknowledgment of the right to a sound climate. As ecological difficulties mount, the crossing point between basic freedoms and natural security turns out to be progressively clear. The right to a solid climate highlights the interconnectedness of biological prosperity and human thriving. Ecological debasement, environmental change, and contamination present dangers not exclusively to biological systems yet additionally to the acknowledgment of different common freedoms, including the right to life, wellbeing, and a sufficient way of life.

The rule of intergenerational value builds up the drawn out point of view inborn in basic liberties. It recognizes that the advantages of privileges ought to be passed down to people in the future, requiring mindful and supportable stewardship of assets. Intergenerational value is especially significant with regards to ecological supportability, where present activities have significant ramifications for the prosperity of people in the future.

The worldwide legitimate structure for basic freedoms contains an intricate embroidery of settlements, shows, and standard global regulation. The Worldwide Bill of Basic freedoms, comprising of the UDHR, the ICCPR, and the Global Agreement on Financial, Social and Social Privileges (ICESCR), structures the foundation of worldwide common liberties regulation. Local common liberties instruments, for example, the European Show on Basic freedoms and the African Contract on Human and People groups' Privileges, supplement the worldwide structure by tending to area explicit difficulties and needs.

Worldwide basic liberties components assume a significant part in observing and implementing consistence with common freedoms norms. Settlement bodies, for example, the Common liberties Board of trustees and the Advisory group on the End of Racial Segregation, audit state reports and issue suggestions to improve privileges insurance. Exceptional rapporteurs, named by the Unified Countries Basic liberties Committee, research and report on unambiguous common freedoms issues, adding to the worldwide talk on privileges advancement and insurance.

The Worldwide Crook Court (ICC) addresses a milestone improvement in the journey for responsibility for deplorable basic freedoms infringement. Laid out by the Rome Rule, the ICC has the locale to arraign people for wrongdoings like slaughter, atrocities, and violations against humankind. The ICC typifies the global local area's obligation to finishing exemption for those liable for the gravest denials of basic liberties.

Regardless of the strong worldwide legitimate system, the execution of basic freedoms stays a perplexing and diverse test. State sway, political contemplations, and power elements frequently obstruct viable privileges insurance. Common liberties infringement continue in different areas of the planet, going from furnished clashes and tyrant systems to foundational separation and social imbalances.

The standard of obligation to safeguard (R2P) addresses a change in outlook in tending to mass monstrosities and grave denials of basic freedoms. Embraced by the global local area at the 2005 World Culmination, R2P declares that states have an obligation to shield their populaces from slaughter, atrocities, ethnic purifying, and wrongdoings against humankind. In circumstances where states clearly neglect to safeguard their residents, the global local area is called upon to mediate, with military power considered if all else fails.

The difficulties to the execution of common freedoms additionally stretch out to the domain of financial globalization. While globalization has worked with financial development and mechanical progression, it has likewise led to worries about work double-dealing, natural corruption, and monetary disparities. The basic freedoms structure gives a basic focal point through which to survey the effect of globalization on people and networks, supporting for strategies that focus on human prosperity over simply financial contemplations.

All in all, a top to bottom examination of the center standards basic common liberties uncovers a diverse and interconnected structure that rises above fleeting, social, and international limits. The basic rule of human poise, combined with the all inclusiveness, resoluteness, and relationship of freedoms, shapes the moral bedrock whereupon the common liberties building stands. Philosophical practices, legitimate instruments, and global components all in all add to the powerful development and utilization of basic liberties in a steadily impacting world.

The common liberties venture is set apart by progress and difficulties, accomplishments and mishaps. The continuous battle for privileges insurance requires an immovable obligation to the rules that support this all inclusive structure. As social orders wrestle with complex issues going from mechanical progressions to natural manageability, the persevering through importance of common liberties lies in their ability to adjust and answer the developing shapes of the human experience. As we explore the intricacies of the 21st 100 years, the standards hidden common freedoms give both.

3.2 Equality, dignity, and freedom as fundamental pillars

Balance, pride, and opportunity stand as major support points in the structure of basic liberties, shaping the bedrock whereupon the whole system rests. These standards are not simple dynamic ideas; rather, they address the pith of living in an equitable and sympathetic culture. An investigation of every one of these support points uncovers their interconnectedness and their significant effect on molding the forms of common freedoms talk.

At the core of the common freedoms system lies the guideline of equity. This standard attests that each individual is qualified for similar thought and security of their freedoms, paying little heed to variables like race, orientation, religion, or financial status.

The Widespread Statement of Common liberties (UDHR), a basic report in the domain of basic liberties, broadcasts in its most memorable article that "all people are conceived free and rise to in pride and privileges." This announcement lays out fairness as a foundation, stressing that the acknowledgment of shared humankind goes before any differentiations or divisions.

Balance goes past a basic statement of similarity; it requests the disposal of oppressive practices and the making of conditions that guarantee reasonableness and equity for all. The standard of non-segregation is complicatedly woven into different common freedoms instruments, mirroring a promise to destroying obstructions that sustain imbalance. Peaceful accords, like the Show on the Disposal of All Types of Victimization Ladies (CEDAW) and the Show on the Freedoms of People with Incapacities (CRPD), typify the worldwide goal to make an existence where people are not exposed to segregation based on innate qualities.

The idea of balance likewise meets with the possibility of value, perceiving that treating everybody the very same may not be guaranteed to bring about reasonableness. Value recognizes that authentic treacheries and foundational disparities require designated measures and governmental policy regarding minorities in society to guarantee that the advantages of common freedoms are open to all, regardless of their beginning stage. This nuanced approach plans to review verifiable wrongs and make everything fair, lining up with the all-encompassing objective of uniformity.

Respect, one more major mainstay of basic freedoms, is well established in the acknowledgment of the intrinsic worth of each and every person. The UDHR, in its prelude, pronounces that "acknowledgment of the innate nobility and of the equivalent and unavoidable privileges of all individuals from the human family is the groundwork of opportunity, equity and harmony on the planet." Respect fills in as the wellspring from which basic freedoms stream, underlining that every individual has an essential worth that rises above outer conditions.

The idea of human respect is multi-layered, enveloping the independence, organization, and natural worth of people. Independence, with regards to common liberties, alludes to the capacity of people to arrive at conclusions about their own lives liberated from pressure or unnecessary obstruction. The security of independence is apparent in privileges like opportunity of thought, still, small voice, and religion, as well as the right to protection. Poise perceives that people are the best appointed authorities of their own advantages and goals, and basic liberties act as a defensive safeguard against erratic interruption into individual decisions.

Besides, human poise stretches out past individual privileges to include aggregate nobility. Networks, societies, and native people groups likewise reserve a privilege to keep up with their character, customs, and lifestyles. The guideline of social freedoms, as expressed in the Statement on the Privileges of Native People groups, recognizes the significance of safeguarding and advancing the pride of native networks. This acknowledgment highlights that the nobility of people is interwoven with the pride of the networks to which they have a place.

Opportunity, the third mainstay of common liberties, is the key part that ties together uniformity and pride. Opportunity isn't an independent rule yet is unpredictably associated with the acknowledgment of different privileges. The UDHR highlights the relationship of privileges by expressing in its preface that "the appearance of a world where people will appreciate the right to speak freely of discourse and conviction and independence from dread and need has been broadcasted as the most noteworthy yearning of the everyday citizens."

Political opportunity, communicated through privileges like opportunity of articulation, gathering, and affiliation, is essential in the working of popularity based social orders. These freedoms engage people to take part openly talk, express dispute, and consider people with significant influence responsible. The option to take part in the administration of one's nation, as cherished in the Global Pledge on Common and Political Privileges (ICCPR), isn't just a crucial opportunity yet additionally a system for guaranteeing that states are responsible to individuals.

Financial opportunity, appeared justified to work, the right to a sufficient way of life, and the right to instruction, adds to the general prosperity of people and networks. The standards of financial, social, and social privileges perceive that certified opportunity requires something beyond the shortfall of political intimidation; it requires the production of conditions that empower people to lead satisfying and noble lives.

The interconnectedness of these three points of support — uniformity, respect, and opportunity — is apparent in the unbreakable quality and association of basic liberties. Common and political privileges, which protect political opportunities and freedoms, are indivisible from financial, social, and social freedoms, which guarantee the material circumstances for an existence of poise. The right to instruction, for instance, is both a common and political right (opportunity) and a monetary, social, and social right (correspondence and pride). This interchange supports the comprehensive idea of common liberties, stressing that the full acknowledgment of one right improves the acknowledgment of others.

The journey for orientation equity fills in as a powerful outline of the interconnectedness of these support points. Orientation fairness isn't simply a ladies' rights issue however a key common freedoms basic. The Show on the Disposal of All Types of Victimization Ladies (CEDAW) is a milestone instrument that tends to segregation in light of sex and takes a stab at orientation fairness in lawful, political, financial, and social circles. The standards of balance, pride, and opportunity meet in the battle for orientation freedoms, highlighting the connection of these principal points of support.

The standard of uniformity is major to destroying orientation based separation, guaranteeing that ladies and men partake in similar privileges and amazing open doors. Nobility becomes possibly the most important factor by perceiving and regarding the independence and

organization of ladies, asserting their entitlement to settle on decisions about their bodies, lives, and fates. Opportunity is fundamental in testing and destroying cultural standards that propagate orientation generalizations and limit the full support of ladies in all parts of life.

The LGBTQ+ privileges development likewise epitomizes the interconnection of these standards. The battle for fairness for lesbian, gay, sexually unbiased, transsexual, and eccentric people rotates around testing unfair regulations, strategies, and cultural mentalities. Respect is a focal subject, underlining that each person, paying little heed to sexual direction or orientation character, has inborn worth and is qualified for live unafraid of segregation or mistreatment. Opportunity, in this unique circumstance, is about the option to communicate one's personality really and transparently, liberated from cultural bias and legitimate restrictions.

Ecological equity, a squeezing worry in the contemporary basic liberties talk, likewise highlights the combination of uniformity, respect, and opportunity. The right to a solid climate is progressively perceived as indispensable to the acknowledgment of basic liberties. Ecological debasement, contamination, and environmental change excessively influence weak networks, frequently compounding existing imbalances. The standards of fairness request that the weights and advantages of ecological arrangements are evenhandedly appropriated, it are not lopsidedly hurt to guarantee that underestimated gatherings.

Poise is entwined with ecological equity through the acknowledgment that a solid climate is fundamental for the prosperity and pride of people and networks. Admittance to clean air, water, and an economical climate isn't simply a natural concern yet an issue of human nobility. Opportunity becomes possibly the most important factor as natural protectors declare their right to data, investment, and a place of refuge to advocate for the insurance of the climate unafraid of responses.

The battle for racial equity, a persevering and worldwide test, exemplifies the getting through pertinence of equity, nobility, and opportunity. Verifiable traditions of servitude, imperialism, and fundamental bigotry keep on molding the encounters of minimized networks. The standards of equity require the destroying of prejudicial designs and the acknowledgment of the full mankind and privileges, all things considered, regardless of their racial or ethnic foundation.

Poise, with regards to racial equity, is tied in with certifying the value and organization of people from generally underestimated networks. Opportunity is weaved with the option to live liberated from racial segregation, the option to approach amazing open doors, and the option to take part completely in the public arena without confronting foundational hindrances. Developments, for example, People of color Matter feature the interconnected battle for equity, nobility, and opportunity, underscoring that these standards are not dynamic goals but rather dire objectives for equity.

The lawful contraption and establishments that shield common freedoms are basic in making an interpretation of these standards into unmistakable securities for people. Global basic freedoms regulation, with its fundamental reports and shows, gives a regularizing structure that states are committed to maintain. Deals, like the Worldwide Agreement on Common and Political Privileges (ICCPR) and the Global Pledge on Financial, Social and Social Privileges (ICESCR), frame the particular commitments of states in guaranteeing the privileges and opportunities of people.

Public general sets of laws assume an essential part in carrying out and upholding basic freedoms. Established ensures, bills of privileges, and homegrown regulation are the instruments through which states focus on maintaining the standards of uniformity, respect, and opportunity. Autonomous legal authorities and basic freedoms commissions act as minds legislative power, guaranteeing that the privileges of people are safeguarded against inconsistent activities.

Worldwide and territorial basic liberties instruments, like the Unified Countries Common freedoms Committee, the European Court of Common freedoms, and the Between American Court of Common freedoms, add to the implementation of common freedoms guidelines. These bodies survey state consistence with common freedoms arrangements, research claims of infringement, and issue proposals or decisions. Their job is significant in considering states responsible and giving solutions for people whose privileges have been encroached upon.

Non-administrative associations (NGOs) and common society assume an imperative part in supporting for basic freedoms. These entertainers frequently act as guard dogs, pointing out privileges infringement, offering help to casualties, and forcing states to satisfy their basic freedoms commitments. Grassroots developments, activated around issues of uniformity, poise, and opportunity, have generally been impetuses for social change, pushing for lawful changes and cultural change.

Notwithstanding the headway made in the domain of basic liberties, considerable difficulties endure. Dictator systems, furnished clashes, financial disparities, and social biases keep on subverting the standards of uniformity, respect, and opportunity. The ascent of egalitarian developments in different regions of the planet represents a danger to the comprehensiveness and inclusivity of common liberties, as certain pioneers look to shorten privileges securities for the sake of public interest or social particularism.

Innovative headways, while offering uncommon open doors, additionally present moral predicaments that converge with basic freedoms. Issues like computerized observation, security intrusion, and the utilization of man-made reasoning bring up issues about the harmony between mechanical development and the assurance of key freedoms.

The standards of uniformity, poise, and opportunity should direct the moral turn of events and sending of innovation to guarantee that basic liberties are not forfeited at the special raised area of progress.

The continuous battle for common freedoms highlights the requirement for a comprehensive and multifaceted methodology. Perceiving the interconnectedness of different types of segregation and persecution is fundamental for tending to the underlying drivers of common freedoms infringement. The battle for orientation correspondence, for example, should likewise defy issues of racial, financial, and natural equity to make a more comprehensive and just society.

3.3 Illustrating the impact of these principles on societies

The effect of the central standards of fairness, pride, and opportunity on social orders is significant and broad. These standards, revered in common freedoms structures around the world, act as the ethical compass and directing light for building just, comprehensive, and flourishing networks. Analyzing their effect on social orders requires diving into explicit settings, going from civil rights developments to strategy executions, to comprehend how these standards shape the texture of our aggregate presence.

Correspondence, as a primary guideline, is an impetus for extraordinary change inside social orders. It requests the destroying of fundamental hindrances that propagate separation and minimization. In the domain of training, the guideline of equity declares that each person, no matter what their experience, merits admittance to quality learning potential open doors. This has provoked endeavors to address instructive abberations, both at the public and global levels. Drives pointed toward giving grants, advancing comprehensive educational programs, and guaranteeing equivalent admittance to instructive assets are meaningful of the obligation to uniformity's groundbreaking potential.

In the work environment, the rule of balance appears in attempts to take out orientation based wage holes, advance variety and consideration, and destroy unfair practices. Arrangements upholding for equivalent compensation for equivalent work, breaking unreasonable impediments for underrepresented gatherings, and cultivating comprehensive corporate societies represent the cultural effect of the fairness standard. The acknowledgment that variety is a resource instead of an obligation is reshaping hierarchical designs and adding to additional fair and imaginative social orders.

The LGBTQ+ freedoms development gives a powerful delineation of the extraordinary effect of the balance standard. Backing for the freedoms of lesbian, gay, sexually open, transsexual, and eccentric people has tested prejudicial regulations, approaches, and cultural perspectives.

The push for marriage uniformity, hostile to separation regulations, and comprehensive medical services strategies mirrors a more extensive cultural shift towards perceiving and confirming the equivalent freedoms of people no matter what their sexual direction or orientation personality. This development exhibits that the standards of fairness safeguard the privileges of explicit gatherings as well as add to reshaping cultural standards and mentalities.

Nobility, as a core value, is a power for social and cultural change. With regards to law enforcement frameworks, the rule of respect requires the compassionate treatment of people, even those blamed or indicted for violations. Endeavors to change correctional and dehumanizing rehearses inside jails, advocate for helpful equity, and guarantee admittance to restoration programs represent the cultural effect of the poise rule. These drives perceive the inborn worth of each and every person, even notwithstanding lawful offenses, and look to make frameworks that maintain human poise.

The guideline of pride is additionally essential to medical care frameworks, impacting approaches and practices that focus on persistent independence, informed assent, and admittance to stately clinical consideration. Palliative consideration, for example, accentuates the help of actual enduring as well as the protection of patients' poise even with difficult disease. The acknowledgment that medical care isn't just about treating sicknesses yet additionally about protecting the poise of people mirrors a significant change in cultural perspectives toward additional humane and patient-focused approaches.

Natural equity, educated by the rule regarding pride, highlights the interconnectedness between human prosperity and environmental equilibrium. Cultural developments upholding for natural maintainability and environment equity perceive that a solid climate is fundamental for the nobility and prosperity of networks. Endeavors to address ecological prejudice, where underestimated networks endure the worst part of natural dangers, represent the cultural effect of the poise standard. The call for reasonable practices and the assurance of biological systems mirrors a comprehension that the poise of people is characteristically connected to the wellbeing of the planet.

Opportunity, as a core value, enables people and social orders to challenge harsh designs and backer for equity. In the domain of common freedoms, the opportunity of articulation fills in as a foundation for majority rule social orders. Cultural developments, whether upholding for political change, civil rights, or basic liberties, depend on the opportunity to voice disagree, scrutinize frameworks, and prepare networks. The effect of opportunity on social orders is apparent in the groundbreaking force of grassroots developments that have started social change, brought down harsh systems, and high level the reason for equity.

The battle for press opportunity is symbolic of how the opportunity rule molds social orders. A free and free media fills in as a guard dog, considering people with great influence responsible and giving residents crucial data.

Cultural developments pushing for press opportunity oppose restriction, battle deception, and add to the making of educated and engaged networks. The effect of a free press reaches out past individual freedoms to the wellbeing of majority rule organizations and the flexibility of social orders against tyrant inclinations.

Political opportunity, appeared through the ok to partake in the administration of one's nation, significantly affects social orders. The foundation and security of vote based organizations guarantee that people have something to do with the choices that influence their lives. Social orders that focus on political opportunity put resources into components like free and fair decisions, partition of abilities, and law and order. These instruments add to stable administration, social union, and the insurance of basic freedoms.

Monetary opportunity, established in standards of correspondence and pride, significantly molds social orders by affecting the circulation of assets and amazing open doors. Endeavors to lessen monetary disparities, give social security nets, and guarantee fair work rehearses mirror a promise to the standards of opportunity. Cultural developments upholding for laborers' privileges, fair exchange rehearses, and financial equity are demonstrative of the extraordinary capability of monetary opportunity. The quest for comprehensive financial arrangements adds to the general prosperity and soundness of social orders.

The diversity of these standards becomes apparent while inspecting the effect on powerless and minimized networks. Native privileges, for example, exemplify the interconnectedness of balance, respect, and opportunity. Endeavors to perceive and safeguard the freedoms of native people groups frequently include testing authentic treacheries, advancing social conservation, and guaranteeing the right to self-assurance. The effect on social orders isn't just the insurance of explicit freedoms however the encouraging of assorted and comprehensive social scenes that commend the lavishness of human societies.

In post-struggle social orders, the standards of equity, pride, and opportunity assume a crucial part in remaking broke networks. Temporary equity processes, pointed toward tending to past denials of basic liberties, underline responsibility, compensations, and compromise. The cultural effect of these standards is clear in the recuperating and reconstructing of networks destroyed by struggle. The acknowledgment of the freedoms of casualties, the foundation of truth and compromise commissions, and endeavors to guarantee law and order add to the rebuilding of social texture.

The effect of these standards isn't bound to legitimate and strategy systems; it saturates social accounts and cultural mentalities. Cultural acknowledgment of variety, consideration, and the acknowledgment of the innate worth of each and every individual are characteristic of the standards of equity, poise, and opportunity flourishing in the shared mindset. Imaginative articulations, writing, and media that challenge generalizations and supporter for basic freedoms add to the change of cultural standards and stories.

Nonetheless, the effect of these standards isn't unidirectional, and challenges continue. Tyrant systems, cultural biases, and foundational disparities keep on sabotaging the acknowledgment of these standards in different settings. The battle for orientation correspondence, for instance, faces opposition from profoundly imbued male centric designs and social standards. The interconnection of segregation, where people face numerous types of persecution, requires nuanced and multifaceted ways to deal with address the main drivers of imbalance and treachery.

Ecological corruption, energized by unreasonable practices, represents a danger to the pride and prosperity of networks, especially those on the cutting edges of environmental change. The standard of opportunity is tried in social orders where legislatures confine city space, reduce opportunity of articulation, or subvert majority rule foundations. The battle for financial equity go on as social orders wrestle with issues of pay disparity, shifty work rehearses, and monetary frameworks that propagate foundational treacheries.

Chapter 4

Challenges and Controversies

In the huge scene of human life, difficulties and debates are woven into the texture of our aggregate insight. These components, frequently natural for progress and advancement, shape the course of social orders, societies, and people. From the beginning of progress to the current day, humankind has explored a complicated snare of difficulties, igniting contentions that test the restrictions of our figuring out, resistance, and versatility.

One of the perpetual difficulties looked by humankind is the mission for information and truth. The quest for understanding the universe and our place in it has prompted logical forward leaps, philosophical upsets, and mechanical headways. However, this journey isn't without its difficulties. The actual idea of investigation and revelation welcomes vulnerability and the unexplored world. Logical contentions emerge as hypotheses conflict, standards shift, and the limits of human information are driven further.

One such contention is the continuous discussion among creationism and development. The conflict between strict convictions and logical proof has energized a well established fight, setting confidence in opposition to reason. While science tries to unwind the secrets of our beginnings through exact perception and examination, strict precepts offer elective accounts that frequently challenge logical clarifications. This conflict has prompted hostile discussions in instructive settings, courts, and public gatherings, featuring the strain between strict opportunity and the logical technique.

The difficulties stretch out past the domain of conceptual thoughts and into the useful field of cultural association. The consistently developing nature of human social orders presents a steady battle to offset individual privileges with everyone's benefit. Issues like security, opportunity of articulation, and the constraints of government authority become landmarks where contending values and interests impact.

Security, when thought about an essential right, faces extraordinary difficulties in the computerized age. The fast headway of innovation has introduced a time where individual data is both an important ware and a likely danger. The omnipresence of reconnaissance cameras, online entertainment stages, and information mining rehearses raises worries about the disintegration of individual security. State run administrations and organizations use gigantic power in gathering, examining, and taking advantage of individual information, igniting banters about the compromise among security and protection.

Additionally, the idea of opportunity of appearance faces difficulties in the time of falsehood and web-based entertainment. The democratization of data sharing stages has engaged people to voice their viewpoints on a worldwide scale. Nonetheless, this newly discovered opportunity has additionally brought about the spread of deception, disdain discourse, and online provocation. The pressure between the option to communicate one's thoughts and the need to diminish hurtful substance places social orders in a fragile difficult exercise, wrestling with the obligation of directing web-based spaces without encroaching on free discourse.

The job of government in managing and shaping social orders is an enduring wellspring of contention. Inquiries regarding the proper extent of government intercession, the harmony between individual freedoms and aggregate government assistance, and the appropriation of assets fuel continuous discussions. Financial philosophies, like free enterprise and communism, support these conversations, forming arrangements that influence the dissemination of abundance, admittance to open doors, and the general prosperity of residents.

Free enterprise, with its accentuation on unregulated economies and confidential undertaking, has been a main impetus behind monetary development and advancement. Notwithstanding, it likewise brings up issues about pay imbalance, double-dealing, and the grouping of abundance in the possession of a couple.

The quest for benefit frequently conflicts with social and ecological worries, prompting banters about the moral obligations of organizations and the requirement for administrative systems to guarantee fair practices.

On the opposite finish of the range, communism advocates for a more impartial circulation of assets and open doors. The pressure between individual drive and aggregate liability characterizes the talk on the job of the state in offering social types of assistance, directing ventures, and tending to fundamental disparities. The authentic instances of communist examinations and their results add to the continuous discussion encompassing the reasonability and supportability of such financial models.

The difficulties looked by social orders are not restricted to homegrown issues; they stretch out to the worldwide stage, where countries wrestle with complex international elements. The quest for public interests, regional debates, and the journey for power make an unpredictable blend of difficulties that test the conciliatory abilities and key discernment of world pioneers.

One of the most squeezing worldwide difficulties is the issue of environmental change. The logical agreement on human-initiated environmental change has prompted pressing calls for aggregate activity to alleviate its effect. In any case, the reaction to this challenge is muddled by monetary interests, international competitions, and the trouble of organizing endeavors on a worldwide scale. Discussions emerge over the distribution of obligation, the job of created and non-industrial countries, and the compromises between monetary development and natural maintainability.

In the domain of global relations, clashes and emergencies frequently arise because of verifiable complaints, contending belief systems, and fights for control. The Center East, with its complicated embroidery of societies, religions, and international interests, remains as a demonstration of the getting through difficulties of accomplishing dependability and harmony. The Israeli-Palestinian struggle, provincial competitions, and the effect of outside intercessions make an unstable scene where political arrangements stay tricky.

The difficulties looked by mankind additionally stretch out to the space of general wellbeing, as confirmed by the continuous worldwide fight against irresistible sicknesses. The development of novel infections, like the Coronavirus pandemic, features the weakness of worldwide wellbeing frameworks and the requirement for facilitated reactions. Discussions encompassing general wellbeing measures, antibody dissemination, and the job of worldwide associations highlight the fragile harmony between individual opportunities and the aggregate prosperity of social orders.

The crossing point of science and morals is a rich ground for contentions that bring up basic issues about the limits of human information and the moral ramifications of mechanical headways.

The area of biotechnology, for instance, presents phenomenal conceivable outcomes and difficulties as researchers investigate hereditary designing, cloning, and other extraordinary innovations.

The moral problem encompassing hereditary altering, exemplified by the CRISPR-Cas9 innovation, outlines the intricacy of exploring the possibility to fix hereditary infections against the dangers of unseen side-effects. Inquiries concerning the ethical obligation of researchers, the ramifications of changing the human germline, and the requirement for worldwide guidelines highlight the difficulties of outfitting the force of biotechnology while guaranteeing moral norms.

The domain of man-made reasoning (simulated intelligence) presents its own arrangement of difficulties and discussions. The quick advancement of simulated intelligence innovations, including AI and independent frameworks, raises worries about work uprooting, security attack, and the potential for one-sided navigation. The moral contemplations of simulated intelligence applications in regions like medical services, law enforcement, and fighting incite banters about responsibility, straightforwardness, and the requirement for moral structures to direct the turn of events and organization of these advances.

Social issues, well established in social standards and verifiable heritages, add to getting through difficulties and debates that shape the elements of social orders. The battle for orientation correspondence, for example, rises above geographic and social limits, appearing in banters about equivalent compensation, regenerative privileges, and portrayal in different fields. The #MeToo development, filled by disclosures of inappropriate behavior and attack, highlights the inescapable idea of orientation based separation and the continuous battle for equity and responsibility.

Race and nationality keep on being quarrelsome issues, with social orders wrestling with the tradition of expansionism, subjection, and foundational prejudice. Banters about governmental policy regarding minorities in society, repayments, and the acknowledgment of authentic treacheries feature the difficulties of accomplishing racial value and cultivating comprehensive social orders. The People of color Matter development, conceived out of the need to address police brutality and fundamental prejudice, represents the force of grassroots activism in driving discussions about civil rights.

Strict and social contentions add one more layer of intricacy to the embroidery of human difficulties. The conflict of values and convictions, whether inside a general public or between various societies, powers banters about social appointment, strict opportunity, and the harmony between social safeguarding and progress. The strain among secularism and strict traditionalism works out in issues, for example, the option to swear, the acknowledgment of LGBTQ+ freedoms, and the job of strict foundations in molding public approaches.

The domain of schooling isn't resistant to difficulties and discussions, as it wrestles with inquiries regarding educational plan content, showing techniques, and the job of teachers in shaping the personalities of the future. The discussion over state sanctioned testing, for instance, brings up issues about value, access, and the viability of assessing a different scope of understudies through a normalized focal point. The pressure between scholastic opportunity and the requirement for normalized appraisals highlights the difficulties of making a comprehensive and successful school system.

Mechanical headways in training, like web based learning stages and man-made reasoning applications, present new difficulties and contentions. The advanced gap, portrayed by variations in admittance to innovation and the web, worsens existing imbalances in instructive open doors. The moral contemplations of information protection, the effect of innovation on human association, and the job of simulated intelligence in evaluating and appraisal incite continuous discussions about the eventual fate of schooling.

The difficulties and contentions implanted in the texture of human life are not exclusively outside powers; they likewise manifest inside people as they wrestle with inquiries of character, reason, and profound quality. The quest for significance and satisfaction frequently prompts existential difficulties that rise above social, strict, and cultural limits.

The convergence of science and otherworldliness, for instance, brings up issues about the similarity of strict convictions with logical revelations. The deep rooted struggle among creationism and advancement mirrors the more extensive strain among confidence and reason, provoking people to accommodate their profound convictions with the experimental proof given by logical request. The quest for an agreeable blend of science and otherworldliness stays a continuous excursion for some, featuring the intricacy of exploring the domains of the known and the unexplored world.

Emotional well-being, one more component of individual prosperity, presents its own arrangement of difficulties and contentions. The shame encompassing emotional wellness issues, combined with restricted admittance to assets and backing, makes hindrances to looking for help. Banters about the medicalization of emotional well-being, the job of drug mediations, and the requirement for all encompassing methodologies highlight the difficulties of tending to the complex and nuanced nature of mental prosperity.

The difficulties and discussions innate in the human experience act as cauldrons for development, strength, and cultural advancement. As people and social orders explore these mind boggling scenes, they are stood up to with decisions that shape the direction of their aggregate process. The strain among custom and progress, individual freedoms and aggregate liabilities, and the known and the obscure moves humankind forward, fashioning a way that is however flighty as it seems to be significant.

4.1 Discussion of contemporary challenges to human rights

In the 21st hundred years, the talk encompassing basic freedoms has become progressively perplexing and complex, as contemporary difficulties test the strength and adequacy of laid out systems. Common liberties, thought about widespread and natural, are planned to defend the pride, opportunity, and balance, everything being equal. Nonetheless, the developing scene of worldwide governmental issues, innovation, and cultural elements has led to new difficulties that request a basic assessment of existing standards and practices.

One of the first difficulties to basic liberties in the contemporary time is the ascent of tyranny and the disintegration of majority rule establishments. In different regions of the planet, pioneers with imperious propensities have looked to merge power, subvert law and order, and stifle contradict. The abbreviation of political opportunities, limitations on the media, and the utilization of state contraption for political mistreatment present critical dangers to the crucial standards of basic liberties.

The disintegration of vote based standards is especially apparent in the rising polarization of social orders and the control of data in the advanced age. The multiplication of web-based entertainment stages has made protected, closed off areas that build up existing convictions and cultivate disinformation. This pattern sabotages the popularity based beliefs of an educated and drew in populace, making it trying to cultivate open and productive discourse on issues that influence common freedoms.

Besides, the weaponization of innovation by tyrant systems raises worries about observation, protection, and oversight. State-supported cyberattacks, computerized reconnaissance, and the utilization of trend setting innovations for social control have huge ramifications for individual opportunities. The strain between mechanical headways and the security of common freedoms highlights the requirement for moral contemplations and global participation to lay out standards overseeing the utilization of innovation in manners that regard human pride and independence.

In the domain of common freedoms, the right to protection faces phenomenal difficulties in the computerized age. Mass observation programs, both by legislatures and confidential elements, raise worries about the degree and meddling of information assortment. The omnipresence of reconnaissance cameras, the following of online exercises, and the assortment of individual data for business purposes make a scene where the limits among public and confidential circles become progressively obscured.

The rise of observation innovations, for example, facial acknowledgment adds another aspect to the conversation, as it can possibly affect opportunity of development and namelessness. The utilization of such advances by policing different elements brings up issues about the harmony between open security and individual protection.

Finding some kind of harmony requires a nuanced approach that considers the potential for misuse and the need to shield people from unjustifiable interruptions into their confidential lives.

With regards to computerized security, the assortment and abuse of individual information by tech organizations have become essential issues of conflict. The plans of action of numerous internet based stages depend on the adaptation of client information through designated publicizing. While these practices drive the computerized economy, they likewise bring up moral issues about assent, information proprietorship, and the potential for control. The pressure between the financial interests of tech organizations and the insurance of individual protection features the requirement for hearty administrative systems that focus on the freedoms and organization of clients.

The approach of man-made consciousness (artificial intelligence) further muddles the scene of basic freedoms, acquainting moral issues and difficulties with laid out legitimate structures. The utilization of computer based intelligence in dynamic cycles, for example, prescient policing, business screening, and law enforcement, raises worries about predisposition, separation, and the absence of straightforwardness. The darkness of simulated intelligence calculations and the potential for building up existing social disparities present critical difficulties to the standards of fairness and non-segregation.

Also, the advancement of independent weapons frameworks, including drones and deadly man-made intelligence controlled machines, brings up moral and legitimate issues about responsibility and the right to life. The potential for these advances to be utilized in furnished clashes without human mediation challenges laid out standards of worldwide compassionate regulation. The global local area wrestles with the requirement for guidelines that administer the turn of events and utilization of independent weapons, guaranteeing adherence to rules that defend common liberties in the midst of contention.

Movement and displaced person emergencies present one more arrangement of difficulties to basic liberties in the contemporary world. Relocation, whether brought about by struggle, abuse, or ecological elements, seriously endangers people and networks of common liberties infringement. The treatment of travelers and exiles, especially at lines and confinement offices, is a point of convergence of concern. Issues like family partition, lacking everyday environments, and forswearing of essential privileges request consideration and activity from the worldwide local area.

The ascent of xenophobia and hostile to settler feelings in different regions of the planet adds a layer of intricacy to the security of basic freedoms for transients. The way of talking of rejection and the execution of prohibitive migration arrangements sabotage the standards of equity and non-separation. The worldwide reaction to relocation challenges requires an exhaustive and cooperative methodology that focuses on the nobility and prosperity of people progressing.

Contemporary difficulties to common freedoms additionally converge with issues of monetary imbalance and civil rights. The hole between the rich and poor people, both inside and between nations, stays a constant test that has colossal ramifications for common freedoms. Monetary differences add to inconsistent admittance to schooling, medical care, and potential open doors for social versatility, propagating patterns of neediness and minimization.

The option to work and fair work rehearses are essential parts of common freedoms that face continuous difficulties in the contemporary monetary scene. The gig economy, portrayed by dubious and non-standard business, brings up issues about employer stability, advantages, and laborers' freedoms. The disintegration of conventional business structures and the gigification of work make a requirement for versatile legitimate systems that guarantee the security of laborers in a quickly changing work market.

Civil rights developments, like the battle against racial shamefulness and police ruthlessness, bring to the very front foundational challenges that obstruct the acknowledgment of basic liberties for all. The unbalanced effect of policing on minimized networks highlights the requirement for changes that address foundational prejudice and advance responsibility. The People of color Matter development, among others, advocates for a reconsideration of policing techniques, law enforcement strategies, and the destroying of designs that propagate disparity.

Orientation equity, in spite of progress in numerous region, stays an unavoidable test to basic freedoms. Segregation, savagery, and provocation in light of orientation keep on upsetting the full cooperation of ladies and orientation minorities in different circles of life. The MeToo development and different drives feature the predominance of inappropriate behavior and attack, requesting a social shift and foundational changes to guarantee the insurance of people from orientation based savagery and separation.

Issues connected with conceptive freedoms and LGBTQ+ privileges further highlight the intricacies of common liberties in contemporary society. Discusses encompassing admittance to conceptive medical care, including early termination freedoms, bring up issues about substantial independence and the option to settle on conclusions around one's own body. Likewise, the battle for LGBTQ+ privileges envelops issues like marriage balance, against segregation regulations, and the acknowledgment of different orientation characters. The strain between conventional standards and developing cultural mentalities requires a cautious route of social responsive qualities while maintaining the standards of equity and non-segregation.

Ecological debasement and the effect of environmental change present interconnected difficulties that have suggestions for common freedoms. The unfriendly impacts of environmental change, including outrageous climate occasions, rising ocean levels, and asset shortage, lopsidedly influence weak networks. The right to a sound climate, clean water, and sufficient lodging turns out to be progressively tricky notwithstanding ecological corruption.

Native people group, frequently on the forefronts of ecological emergencies, face one of a kind difficulties to their freedoms, including land privileges and social safeguarding. The double-dealing of regular assets, deforestation, and the infringement of ventures into native domains worsen existing imbalances and compromise the social legacy of native people groups. Tending to the crossing point of natural equity and common liberties requires a comprehensive methodology that perceives the interconnectedness of biological supportability and human prosperity.

With regards to general wellbeing, the worldwide reaction to pandemics, for example, the Coronavirus emergency presents difficulties to common liberties that require a sensitive harmony between open security and individual opportunities. Measures like lockdowns, quarantine, and contact following bring up issues about the limitation of development, protection concerns, and the potential for segregation. The impartial circulation of immunizations and admittance to medical care further feature the requirement for global participation and a rights-based way to deal with general wellbeing.

4.2 Cultural relativism, political resistance, and other obstacles

Social relativism, political obstruction, and a heap of different hindrances present imposing difficulties to the widespread application and security of basic liberties. These obstructions, established in different social, political, and social settings, highlight the complicated idea of basic liberties talk and the troubles in laying out a worldwide agreement on central standards.

Social relativism, frequently placed as a philosophical point of view, battles that the legitimacy of virtues is dependent upon social setting. In the domain of common liberties, this idea leads to banters about the comprehensiveness of specific privileges and the degree to which social variety ought to be obliged in worldwide basic freedoms structures. While advocates contend that social relativism regards different customs and values, pundits affirm that it tends to be utilized to legitimize rehearses that encroach upon key common liberties, for example, orientation based separation, genital mutilation, or limitations on opportunity of articulation.

The conflict between social relativism and the comprehensiveness of basic freedoms is especially apparent in issues like the privileges of ladies and LGBTQ+ people. In certain societies, profoundly imbued male centric standards propagate orientation based segregation, restricting the privileges and valuable open doors accessible to ladies. Practices like kid marriage, honor killings, and female genital mutilation are in many cases shielded on social relativist grounds, making a strain between regarding social variety and protecting the privileges and respect of people, particularly ladies and orientation minorities.

Essentially, the freedoms of LGBTQ+ people face difficulties in societies that defame and condemn non-heteronormative characters. Social relativism can be conjured to contend against perceiving and safeguarding LGBTQ+ privileges, sustaining separation and brutality.

The pressure between social independence and the basic to safeguard the freedoms of underestimated bunches brings up significant moral and philosophical issues about the job of social relativism in forming global common liberties guidelines.

Political obstruction addresses one more critical deterrent to the acknowledgment of common freedoms. Dictator systems, driven by political plans and a longing to keep up with power, frequently take part in orderly infringement of common liberties. Suppression of political resistance, oversight of free articulation, and the utilization of power against dissidents are normal strategies utilized by state run administrations impervious to vote based standards and common liberties standards.

The concealment of difference and political resistance represents an immediate test to one side to opportunity of articulation and gathering. Writers, activists, and common residents who look to voice their interests or censure government arrangements frequently face oppression, detainment, or even viciousness. The smothering of political dispute sabotages the standards of a vote based system and common liberties, establishing conditions where responsibility and law and order are compromised.

Political opposition isn't restricted to despotic systems; even in justly chosen legislatures, difficulties to basic freedoms can emerge. Egalitarian developments that exploit social divisions and take part in scapegoating can sabotage the assurance of minority privileges. The disintegration of vote based establishments, assaults on the freedom of the legal executive, and endeavors to reduce the privileges of political rivals all add to an environment where common liberties are in danger.

The worldwide ascent of populism and patriot developments further confounds the scene of basic freedoms. Pioneers who appeal to nativist feelings frequently advance strategies that focus on the interests of a specific ethnic or public gathering over the privileges of minorities and transients. The belittling of "the other" and the dismissal of global collaboration can prompt approaches that disregard standards of equity, non-segregation, and the option to look for refuge.

In the domain of monetary privileges, neoliberal financial arrangements and globalization have created their own arrangement of difficulties. Financial disparity, exacerbated by neoliberalism, subverts the acknowledgment of financial privileges, including the option to work, training, and medical care. Severity estimates forced for the sake of financial effectiveness can excessively influence weak populaces, intensifying neediness and restricting admittance to fundamental administrations.

The commodification of regular assets and the abuse of work in the globalized economy bring up issues about corporate obligation and the security of laborers' privileges.

Transnational partnerships, with huge monetary power and impact, frequently work in conditions where administrative systems are feeble, empowering denials of basic liberties, for example, youngster work, risky working circumstances, and natural debasement.

The obstructions to common liberties additionally cross with issues of racial and ethnic separation. Primary bigotry, profoundly imbued in authentic heritages and fundamental disparities, presents critical difficulties to the standards of equity and non-separation. Underestimated people group, especially minorities, face lopsided boundaries to training, work, and medical care, featuring the requirement for extensive endeavors to address fundamental prejudice and advance civil rights.

With regards to equipped struggles and safety efforts, common freedoms are much of the time abused all the while assuming a pretense of keeping up with public safety. Counterterrorism endeavors, while pointed toward guaranteeing public security, frequently lead to the disintegration of common freedoms, erratic detainments, and the utilization of torment. The pressure between security goals and the insurance of individual freedoms is a fragile equilibrium that requires cautious thought and adherence to global legitimate norms.

The peculiarity of statelessness presents one more test to basic freedoms, especially the right to ethnicity and the related privileges that accompany it. Stateless people, frequently barred from legitimate securities and fundamental administrations, face an increased weakness to denials of basic liberties. Segregation, absence of admittance to schooling and medical care, and the refusal of opportunity of development are among the results of statelessness, featuring the requirement for coordinated endeavors to address this neglected test.

The global reaction to compassionate emergencies, including outcast and transient streams, uncovers extra snags to the assurance of common liberties. The exile emergency, powered by clashes, abuse, and natural calamities, strains the limit of countries and worldwide associations to give help and maintain the freedoms of uprooted people. The hesitance of certain nations to acknowledge displaced people, combined with the ascent of hostile to migrant opinions, highlights the troubles in cultivating an aggregate obligation to basic freedoms notwithstanding complex international difficulties.

Common liberties infringement with regards to outfitted clashes are intensified by the exemption delighted in by culprits. The inability to consider people responsible for atrocities, slaughter, and wrongdoings against mankind sabotages the standards of equity and law and order. The foundation of global councils, like the Worldwide Crook Court (ICC), addresses a positive move toward responsibility. Nonetheless, challenges continue guaranteeing the collaboration of states and dealing with culprits, particularly when strong entertainers try to sidestep responsibility.

The impediments of worldwide legitimate systems and the particular implementation of basic liberties principles represent extra obstacles to the acknowledgment of general freedoms. The shortfall of a worldwide requirement system with the position to constrain consistence leaves holes in responsibility. Strong countries, frequently invulnerable from indictment because of international contemplations, can act without any potential repercussions, starting a trend that sabotages the believability of global common freedoms systems.

Additionally, the politicization of common freedoms talk by strong entertainers further muddles endeavors to address infringement. The utilization of basic liberties as a device for political influence or specific mediation can sabotage the authenticity of the common freedoms plan. The strain between the comprehensiveness of basic liberties and the international interests of states requires steady cautiousness to forestall instrumentalization and guarantee reliable application across assorted settings.

The difficulties to basic freedoms are not restricted to the activities of states; non-state entertainers, including furnished gatherings, fanatic associations, and global enterprises, likewise assume critical parts in executing manhandles. The absence of clear lawful systems and components for considering non-state entertainers responsible makes a hole in the security of common liberties. Endeavors to lay out responsibility components for non-state entertainers face critical obstacles, as confirmed by the difficulties in tending to corporate complicity in denials of basic freedoms.

Tending to these diverse difficulties requires a far reaching and cooperative methodology. Endeavors to advance common liberties schooling, mindfulness, and support assume a urgent part in cultivating a culture of regard for human nobility and freedoms. Common society associations, basic freedoms protectors, and grass-roots developments add to the perceivability of common liberties issues and consider legislatures and other strong elements responsible.

Worldwide participation and discretionary endeavors stay fundamental in addressing difficulties to basic liberties at a worldwide scale. Multilateral establishments, like the Assembled Countries and territorial bodies, give gatherings to exchange, discussion, and the plan of standards. Arrangements, shows, and arrangements lay out lawful structures that set guidelines for the insurance of basic freedoms.

4.3 Exploration of controversial issues within the human rights discourse

The basic liberties talk, while established in the standards of comprehensiveness, correspondence, and poise, is a long way from a solid and uncontested field. Questionable issues inside this talk feature the intricacies and difficulties intrinsic chasing a typical system for defending common freedoms. From discusses encompassing social relativism to conversations on the constraints of specific freedoms in unambiguous settings, the investigation of these contentions develops how we might interpret the nuanced idea of common liberties.

Social relativism arises as a critical and persevering through discussion inside the basic freedoms talk. This viewpoint fights that virtues are setting reliant, changing across societies, and hence challenges the possibility of general basic liberties. Advocates contend that social relativism recognizes and regards assorted social customs, underscoring the significance of setting in deciding the legitimacy of moral standards.

Notwithstanding, social relativism has been scrutinized for potential to legitimize rehearses disregard essential basic liberties, especially those connected with orientation equity and individual opportunities. For example, in societies where orientation based separation is profoundly imbued, social relativism may be summoned to legitimize practices like female genital mutilation, youngster marriage, or the subjection of ladies.

The pressure between social relativism and widespread common liberties is especially apparent in issues connected with ladies' privileges. Women's activist developments have long battled against man centric standards and practices that deny ladies equivalent privileges and valuable open doors. The conflict between social independence and the basic to safeguard ladies' privileges brings up significant moral issues about the job of social relativism in molding global common freedoms principles.

One more combative issue inside the basic liberties talk rotates around monetary freedoms and their crossing point with neoliberal financial strategies. While monetary freedoms, including the option to work, training, and a sufficient way of life, are cherished in different worldwide instruments, the neoliberal financial worldview has presented difficulties to their acknowledgment.

Neoliberalism, described by unrestricted economy standards, liberation, and privatization, has been scrutinized for worsening financial disparities and sabotaging social government assistance frameworks. Pundits contend that the quest for benefit and financial development, frequently focused on in neoliberal arrangements, can prompt the disregard of social and monetary privileges, lopsidedly influencing minimized and weak populaces.

The commodification of fundamental administrations, for example, medical services and schooling, under neoliberal systems brings up issues about the prioritization of benefit over human prosperity. The privatization of public administrations, while possibly adding to financial proficiency, can restrict access for the individuals who can't stand to pay, encroaching upon the right to schooling and medical services.

Moreover, financial globalization has prompted the double-dealing of work chasing after upper hands. Transnational organizations, working across borders, may take part in practices, for example, youngster work, unfortunate working circumstances, and natural corruption.

The strain between financial goals and the assurance of laborers' freedoms underlines the requirement for moral contemplations and administrative systems that offset monetary interests with common liberties standards.

The privileges of LGBTQ+ people comprise one more mind boggling and questionable area inside the basic liberties talk. While global basic liberties instruments maintain the standards of correspondence and non-segregation, the privileges of LGBTQ+ people face opposition in different social, strict, and political settings.

In numerous social orders, well established biases and oppressive practices persevere against people who distinguish as LGBTQ+. Criminalization of same-sex connections, separation in work, and viciousness in view of sexual direction or orientation personality stay predominant issues. Debates emerge when endeavors to safeguard LGBTQ+ freedoms conflict with social or strict convictions that view non-heteronormative ways of life as degenerate or indecent.

Banters on LGBTQ+ freedoms stretch out to issues, for example, marriage balance, reception privileges, and the acknowledgment of different orientation characters. The conflict between moderate qualities that supporter for inclusivity and the privileges of LGBTQ+ people and moderate belief systems that oppose social change features the intricacy of adjusting social practices with advancing common liberties standards.

The strain between opportunity of articulation and the counteraction of disdain discourse and segregation is a continuous contention inside the basic liberties talk. While opportunity of articulation is a principal right, the line between safeguarded discourse and destructive discourse that instigates savagery or separation is frequently obscured.

Endeavors to battle disdain discourse and disinformation, especially in the advanced age, bring up issues about as far as possible on opportunity of articulation. The ascent of online stages has worked with the quick spread of disdain discourse, deception, and fanatic philosophies. Adjusting the need to forestall hurt and shield minimized bunches from separation with the option to free articulation presents a considerable test.

Discussions encompassing disdain discourse converge with more extensive discussions on restriction, overt sensitivity, and the job of state run administrations and online stages in managing discourse. Finding some kind of harmony that shields individual opportunities while forestalling the scattering of unsafe substance requires nuanced approaches and a promise to maintaining common freedoms standards.

With regards to furnished clashes, the harmony between public safety objectives and the security of individual privileges turns into a disagreeable issue. Counterterrorism measures, established determined to guarantee public wellbeing, frequently lead to the disintegration of common freedoms, inconsistent detainments, and the utilization of torment.

The strain between security concerns and the insurance of individual freedoms is a sensitive equilibrium that requires cautious thought and adherence to global legitimate principles.

The utilization of observation innovations, both by state entertainers and confidential elements, presents one more disputable aspect inside the basic freedoms talk. While reconnaissance can be legitimate as important for public safety or wrongdoing avoidance, the broad assortment of individual information raises worries about protection, opportunity of articulation, and the potential for misuse.

Mass reconnaissance programs, frequently supported for the sake of counterterrorism endeavors, can encroach upon the right to security. The universality of reconnaissance cameras out in the open spaces, the following of online exercises, and the assortment of individual data for business purposes add to a scene where people might feel continually checked. Finding some kind of harmony between the genuine points of reconnaissance and the assurance of individual freedoms requires vigorous lawful systems, oversight instruments, and moral contemplations.

The moral ramifications of arising innovations, especially computerized reasoning (simulated intelligence), comprise a prospering contention inside the basic liberties talk. The utilization of computer based intelligence in dynamic cycles, for example, prescient policing, business screening, and law enforcement, raises worries about predisposition, separation, and the absence of straightforwardness.

Algorithmic direction, filled by AI, can sustain and try and worsen existing social imbalances. The darkness of computer based intelligence calculations and the potential for prejudicial results present critical difficulties to the standards of balance and non-segregation. Tending to the moral contemplations of simulated intelligence applications in different spaces, including medical care, law enforcement, and reconnaissance, requires progressing discourse, administrative systems, and global participation.

Ecological freedoms and the convergence with basic liberties present a complex and developing debate. The effect of natural corruption, environmental change, and asset double-dealing on human populaces highlights the interconnectedness of ecological privileges and basic freedoms. Weak people group, frequently underestimated and disappointed, endure the worst part of ecological emergencies.

The right to a solid climate, clean water, and reasonable occupations becomes basic even with natural difficulties. Native people group, specifically, face the deficiency of hereditary terrains, social legacy, and conventional lifestyles because of ecological corruption. Discussions emerge when monetary interests, frequently determined by the quest for normal assets, conflict with the freedoms of networks to live in a solid climate.

The strain between the privileges of people in the future and current financial objectives highlights the difficulties in planning strategies that offset ecological supportability with common liberties. Banters about the obligations of states, organizations, and people in moderating environmental change and saving the climate feature the requirement for a comprehensive and privileges based way to deal with ecological issues.

The freedoms of evacuees and transients comprise one more argumentative issue inside the basic liberties talk. Removal, whether brought about by struggle, abuse, or ecological variables, jeopardizes people and networks of common liberties infringement. The treatment of displaced people and travelers, especially at lines and confinement offices, is a point of convergence of concern.

Issues like family detachment, deficient everyday environments, and refusal of fundamental freedoms request consideration and activity from the global local area. The ascent of xenophobia and hostile to outsider feelings in different pieces.

The basic liberties talk addresses a worldwide discussion about the standards, standards, and practices that mean to defend the inborn pride, uniformity, and opportunities of each and every person. Established in the fallout of The Second Great War and the outrages committed during that period, the talk has developed into a perplexing and dynamic field that draws in with an expansive range of issues. From the basic records like the Widespread Statement of Common freedoms to progressing banters about social relativism, financial equity, and arising innovations, the common freedoms talk explores a different territory molded by verifiable, social, political, and social elements.

At its center, the common freedoms talk affirms that specific privileges are general and unavoidable, rising above geographic, social, and political limits. The Widespread Statement of Common liberties, embraced by the Unified Countries General Gathering in 1948, remains as a central record that verbalizes the principal privileges and opportunities to which all people are entitled. These incorporate the right to life, freedom, and security; independence from torment, bondage, and segregation; the option to work, training, and medical care; and the option to take part in government.

Notwithstanding, the comprehensiveness of basic liberties has been a subject of progressing discussion and investigation. Social relativism, as a philosophical viewpoint, challenges that there are all inclusive moral guidelines pertinent to all societies and social orders. Defenders of social relativism contend that virtues are dependent upon social setting, and in this manner, the idea of general common freedoms may not be all around acknowledged.

Social relativism turns out to be especially disagreeable when applied to rehearses that seem to encroach upon key common freedoms. The conflict between social independence and the basic to safeguard individual privileges is most apparent in issues, for example, orientation based segregation, where profoundly imbued social practices might sustain disparity and abuse the standards of orientation balance revered in worldwide common freedoms instruments.

The strain between social relativism and the comprehensiveness of basic liberties is additionally exacerbated in conversations around LGBTQ+ privileges. In numerous social and strict settings, non-heteronormative personalities are slandered or even condemned. Endeavors to advance and safeguard the freedoms of LGBTQ+ people frequently experience opposition grounded in social or strict convictions, showing the perplexing exchange between social independence and basic liberties standards.

Monetary freedoms, fundamental to the common liberties talk, envelop the option to work, training, and a sufficient way of life. In any case, financial belief systems, especially neoliberalism, have introduced difficulties to the acknowledgment of these privileges. Neoliberal strategies, described by unregulated economy standards and liberation, have been scrutinized for worsening monetary disparities and subverting social government assistance frameworks.

The commodification of fundamental administrations, for example, medical care and training, under neoliberal structures brings up issues about the prioritization of benefit over human prosperity. Monetary globalization has prompted the abuse of work in quest for upper hands, and transnational enterprises working in feeble administrative conditions might take part in rehearses that encroach upon laborers' freedoms.

The convergence of monetary privileges with issues of race and nationality further confounds the basic liberties talk. Primary bigotry, profoundly imbued in verifiable heritages and fundamental disparities, presents huge difficulties to the standards of fairness and non-segregation. Minimized people group, especially ethnic minorities, face unbalanced obstructions to training, work, and medical care, featuring the requirement for complete endeavors to address foundational prejudice and advance civil rights.

Opportunity of articulation, a foundation of vote based social orders, is one more component of the common liberties talk that includes complex contemplations. While this right is revered in worldwide basic freedoms instruments, debates emerge while endeavoring to depict the limits between safeguarded discourse and hurtful discourse that actuates brutality or separation.

In the computerized age, the quick spread of disdain discourse, deception, and fanatic belief systems through web-based stages raises worries about the effect on cultural amicability and individual privileges. Finding some kind of harmony between the basic to forestall hurt and safeguard underestimated gatherings and the option to free articulation requires nuanced approaches and a promise to maintaining common liberties standards.

The moral ramifications of arising innovations, especially man-made consciousness (computer based intelligence), have acquainted another aspect with the common liberties talk. The utilization of man-made intelligence in dynamic cycles, for example, prescient policing and law enforcement, raises worries about predisposition, separation, and the absence of straightforwardness.

The murky idea of computer based intelligence calculations and their capability to propagate existing social imbalances present critical difficulties to the standards of balance and non-separation.

Issues connected with protection and observation additionally arise with regards to mechanical headways. Mass observation programs, legitimized for the sake of counter-terrorism endeavors, can encroach upon the right to protection. The universality of reconnaissance cameras, following of online exercises, and assortment of individual data for business purposes add to a scene where the limits among public and confidential circles become progressively obscured.

Ecological privileges, however interconnected with common liberties, present their own arrangement of contentions. The effect of ecological debasement, environmental change, and asset double-dealing on human populaces highlights the need to incorporate natural equity into the common liberties talk. Weak people group, frequently underestimated and disappointed, endure the worst part of natural emergencies, requiring a rights-based way to deal with ecological issues.

The freedoms of exiles and travelers comprise a petulant issue inside the common liberties talk, especially despite expanding worldwide movement streams. Removal, whether brought about by struggle, abuse, or natural elements, seriously endangers people and networks of basic freedoms infringement. Issues like family partition, lacking day to day environments, and forswearing of essential privileges request consideration and activity from the worldwide local area.

Regenerative freedoms, incorporating issues like admittance to contraception, early termination, and maternal medical services, remain profoundly questionable inside the common liberties talk. Banters about the right to life, substantial independence, and the job of government in controlling conceptive decisions feature the conflict between various moral and moral viewpoints.

Debates encompassing regenerative freedoms frequently cross with strict convictions, social standards, and political philosophies. While a supporter for the security of ladies' all in all correct to come to conclusions about their bodies, others contend for the freedoms of the unborn. Arranging a way that regards different points of view while maintaining key freedoms requires cautious thought of moral, lawful, and social aspects.

The basic freedoms talk is additionally tested by the impediments of global legitimate systems and components for implementation. The shortfall of a worldwide requirement system with the power to constrain consistence leaves holes in responsibility. Strong countries, frequently safe from indictment because of international contemplations, can act without risk of punishment, starting a trend that sabotages the validity of global common freedoms instruments.

The politicization of common freedoms talk by strong entertainers adds one more layer of intricacy. The utilization of common freedoms as an instrument for political influence or specific intercession can sabotage the authenticity of the basic liberties plan. The strain between the all inclusiveness of basic freedoms and the international interests of states requires steady cautiousness to forestall instrumentalization and guarantee predictable application across assorted settings.

Non-state entertainers, including equipped gatherings, fanatic associations, and worldwide organizations, additionally add to denials of basic liberties. The absence of clear lawful systems and components for considering non-state entertainers responsible makes a hole in the security of common liberties. Endeavors to lay out responsibility systems for non-state entertainers face huge obstacles, as confirmed by the difficulties in tending to corporate complicity in denials of basic liberties.

Tending to these contentions inside the common freedoms talk requires a thorough and cooperative methodology. Basic liberties training, mindfulness, and support assume a pivotal part in cultivating a culture of regard for human pride and privileges. Common society associations, basic freedoms safeguards, and grassroots developments contribute altogether to the perceivability of common liberties issues and consider states and other strong elements responsible.

Worldwide collaboration and discretionary endeavors stay fundamental in addressing difficulties to basic liberties at a worldwide scale. Multilateral organizations, like the Assembled Countries and territorial bodies, give discussions to discourse, exchange, and the detailing of standards. Deals, shows, and arrangements lay out legitimate structures that set principles for the assurance of basic liberties. The cooperation of states, common society, and different partners in these cycles is urgent to guaranteeing the authenticity and viability of global basic liberties components.

Chapter 5

Human Rights in Action

Basic liberties are crucial rules that shield the intrinsic poise and worth of each and every person. In a world set apart by variety and intricacy, the idea of common freedoms fills in as a general language that rises above lines, societies, and philosophies. It epitomizes the conviction that each individual, no matter what their experience, is qualified for specific natural privileges and opportunities. Common freedoms are not simply unique standards; they track down substantial articulation in the activities and strategies that impact social orders, overall sets of laws, and worldwide relations.

At the core of common liberties is the acknowledgment of the equivalent and natural privileges of all individuals from the human family. This standard, revered in the Widespread Statement of Common liberties embraced by the Unified Countries General Gathering in 1948, establishes the groundwork for a world where equity, opportunity, and respect are stood to each person.

Common freedoms in real life involve the down to earth execution and security of these standards in different features of life, from individual communications to state approaches and worldwide drives.

The right to life remains as a foundation of common freedoms, stressing the intrinsic worth of each and every individual's presence. It stretches out past the short-fall of actual mischief and envelops conditions that permit people to live with poise. Basic freedoms in real life request not just the avoidance of erratic hardship of life yet additionally the making of conditions helpful for the prosperity and thriving of all. This requires resolving issues like destitution, admittance to medical care, and natural maintainability, perceiving their interconnectedness with the right to life.

Opportunity of articulation, an essential basic freedom, enables people to voice their viewpoints, share data, and participate in discourse unafraid of retaliation. Common liberties in real life require the security of this opportunity, as it assumes a critical part in cultivating vote based social orders, informed populace, and social advancement. Be that as it may, the activity of opportunity of articulation isn't without challenges, as it should be offset with liabilities to forestall hurt and maintain the privileges of others.

In the domain of schooling, basic liberties manifest morally justified to get to quality training without segregation. Schooling isn't just a method for procuring information yet additionally an instrument for strengthening, cultivating decisive reasoning, and advancing upsides of resistance and understanding. Guaranteeing equivalent instructive open doors for everything is a fundamental part of basic freedoms in real life, adding to the improvement of comprehensive and impartial social orders.

The option to work is one more fundamental element of basic freedoms, epitomizing the possibility that everybody has the privilege to productive work under and good circumstances. Basic freedoms in real life address issues of work privileges, fair wages, and the destruction of segregation in the work environment. By advancing respectable work, social orders can improve financial soundness, decrease imbalance, and maintain the nobility of people adding to their networks.

Uniformity under the steady gaze of the law is an essential standard of common freedoms, stressing that everybody is qualified for equivalent insurance and advantage of the law without separation. Common freedoms in real life request overall sets of laws that are fair-minded, straightforward, and responsible, guaranteeing that equity is open to all, regardless of their social, financial, or social foundation. Wiping out segregation and inclination from legitimate systems is fundamental for building social orders in light of law and order.

The freedoms of ladies and orientation correspondence are integral to the more extensive common liberties structure. Common liberties in real life require the disposal of segregation in view of orientation, tending to foundational imbalances that persevere in different circles of life. Enabling ladies, guaranteeing their regenerative freedoms, and fighting orientation based viciousness are fundamental parts of common liberties endeavors, adding to the production of social orders where all people can arrive at their maximum capacity.

Basic freedoms reach out to the domain of medical care, incorporating the right to the most noteworthy feasible norm of physical and psychological wellness. Admittance to medical care administrations, disinfection, and safe drinking water are fundamental parts of basic freedoms in real life. Endeavors to address general wellbeing challenges, like pandemics and endemic sicknesses, require a rights-based way to deal with guarantee that wellbeing mediations are evenhanded, open, and conscious of human nobility.

With regards to relocation, basic freedoms in real life request the security of the privileges of transients and outcasts. This incorporates defending their entitlement to look for refuge, shielding them from segregation and abuse, and tending to the main drivers of constrained relocation. Maintaining the privileges of travelers adds to the making of social orders that embrace variety and perceive the commitments of people no matter what their relocation status.

The right to security is a basic part of common liberties in the computerized age. As innovation propels, new difficulties arise in shielding people's protection from outlandish reconnaissance and information breaks. Basic liberties in real life require the advancement of lawful systems and moral norms that safeguard people's protection freedoms while adjusting the advantages of mechanical development.

Basic liberties in struggle zones become particularly significant, as equipped contentions frequently bring about serious infringement of common freedoms. Safeguarding regular people, guaranteeing admittance to helpful guide, and considering culprits responsible are fundamental parts of basic liberties endeavors in struggle circumstances. The worldwide local area assumes a critical part in maintaining common liberties during clashes, through discretionary endeavors, peacekeeping missions, and backing for temporary equity processes.

Ecological privileges have acquired noticeable quality in the talk on basic freedoms, perceiving the interconnectedness between a sound climate and the prosperity of people and networks. Basic freedoms in real life request the security of biological systems, reasonable advancement practices, and endeavors to moderate the effect of environmental change. Incorporating ecological contemplations into basic liberties structures is fundamental for making an existence where people in the future can flourish.

The guideline of non-separation lies at the center of basic freedoms, underlining that everybody is qualified for partake in their privileges without segregation of any sort. Common liberties in real life require endeavors to wipe out separation in light of race, nationality, religion, sexual direction, orientation personality, handicap, and different grounds. Making comprehensive social orders requires testing and destroying foundational hindrances that sustain segregation.

Basic liberties safeguards assume a significant part in propelling common freedoms in real life. They are people, associations, and networks that bravely advocate for the assurance and advancement of common liberties, frequently notwithstanding misfortune. Basic freedoms protectors might confront mistreatment, dangers, and savagery for their work, featuring the significance of worldwide fortitude in supporting their endeavors.

The global local area assumes a critical part in the advancement and security of basic liberties. Deals, shows, and global organizations give a system to collaboration among countries to maintain common liberties principles. Common freedoms in real life expect states to satisfy their commitments under worldwide regulation, participate in tending to worldwide difficulties, and consider each other responsible for basic liberties infringement.

Challenges persevere in the acknowledgment of basic freedoms worldwide. Tyrant systems, political shakiness, monetary imbalance, and social boundaries present snags to the powerful execution of basic liberties in different settings. Basic liberties in real life require supported endeavors to address these difficulties, drawing in with nearby networks, common society, and states to fabricate a culture of regard for common liberties.

All in all, common liberties in real life are not just optimistic beliefs yet a call to change standards into substantial real factors. From the right to life and opportunity of articulation to orientation correspondence and ecological privileges, the range of basic freedoms envelops different aspects of human life. Maintaining common liberties requires aggregate endeavors at the individual, local area, public, and global levels.

It requests a guarantee to equity, correspondence, and pride for all, rising above contrasts and embracing the common mankind that ties us together. Basic liberties in real life are a consistent excursion, set apart by progress, misfortunes, and the unfaltering determination to make an existence where each individual can reside with opportunity, poise, and regard. As people and social orders wrestle with the intricacies of the cutting edge world, the standards of basic freedoms give a compass to explore the way towards an all the more and sympathetic worldwide local area.

5.1 Examining successful implementations of human rights principles

Inspecting effective executions of basic liberties standards uncovers the groundbreaking effect that these standards can have on people, networks, and social orders at large. While challenges continue understanding the full range of basic liberties universally, there are examples where deliberate endeavors have prompted positive results and progressions. These examples of overcoming adversity give significant experiences into the techniques, approaches, and coordinated efforts that add to compelling basic freedoms execution.

One prominent area of achievement is the progression of LGBTQ+ freedoms in different regions of the planet. Throughout the course of recent many years, there has been huge advancement in perceiving and safeguarding the privileges of lesbian, gay, sexually unbiased, transsexual, and eccentric people. Numerous nations have decriminalized same-sex connections, sanctioned enemy of separation regulations, and legitimized same-sex marriage. These lawful changes mirror a more extensive cultural shift towards acknowledgment and inclusivity.

Progress in LGBTQ+ privileges execution frequently results from the energetic endeavors of activists, promotion gatherings, and the impacted networks themselves. Perceivability and mindfulness crusades play had a significant impact in testing generalizations, dispersing legends, and cultivating understanding. Common liberties standards, for example, the option to be liberated from separation and the right to protection, have been critical in outlining the talk and impacting strategy changes.

South Africa stands apart as a contextual investigation in effectively tending to verifiable common freedoms infringement through a momentary equity process. The finish of politically-sanctioned racial segregation in the mid 1990s denoted a defining moment in South Africa's set of experiences. Reality and Compromise Commission (TRC), led by Ecclesiastical overseer Desmond Tutu, was laid out to examine past monstrosities and give a stage to casualties and culprits to share their encounters.

The TRC utilized a helpful equity approach, pointing not exclusively to reveal reality yet in addition to advance compromise and recuperating. Casualties were given a discussion to share their accounts, and culprits could look for pardon by completely unveiling their activities. While the TRC confronted analysis and difficulties, it assumed a significant part in encouraging a feeling of responsibility and giving an establishment to an all the more and comprehensive society.

One more area of fruitful basic liberties execution is found in the domain of handicap freedoms. The Unified Countries Show on the Privileges of People with Handicaps (CRPD), took on in 2006, addresses a milestone global settlement pointed toward advancing, safeguarding, and guaranteeing the full and equivalent satisfaction in basic freedoms by individuals with incapacities.

Nations that have confirmed the CRPD focus on embracing official and strategy measures to kill separation and hindrances looked by people with handicaps. Fruitful execution includes legitimate structures as well as changes in cultural mentalities and the fabricated climate. Available framework, comprehensive training, and work potential open doors are basic parts of understanding the freedoms cherished in the CRPD.

Rwanda's endeavors in post-slaughter compromise and modifying represent a guarantee to common liberties standards in the midst of gigantic difficulties. The decimation in 1994 remaining an overwhelming effect on the country, with a huge number of individuals killed and networks destroyed. In the fallout, Rwanda set out on an excursion of recuperation and compromise.

The Gacaca courts, a local area based equity framework, were laid out to address the staggering number of cases coming about because of the decimation. These courts expected to advance truth-telling, responsibility, and local area mending. While the Gacaca cycle confronted analysis and intricacies, it added to cultivating a feeling of equity and empowering networks to face the past while pursuing a more agreeable future.

In the domain of ladies' privileges, Sweden gives an illustration of effective orientation equity approaches that have pervaded different parts of society. Sweden has reliably positioned high in worldwide orientation balance files, mirroring its obligation to destroying orientation based segregation and advancing ladies' privileges. Strategies like liberal parental leave, reasonable childcare, and endeavors to challenge conventional orientation jobs add to making a more evenhanded society.

The Me Too development, starting in the US yet resounding universally, outlines the force of aggregate activity in testing and uncovering far reaching lewd behavior and attack. The development picked up speed as survivors shared their accounts, prompting a more extensive cultural retribution with issues of force, assent, and responsibility. The Me Too development has provoked changes parents in law, working environment approaches, and social standards, underscoring the significance of common liberties standards in tending to orientation based brutality.

In the field of native privileges, the Maori nation of New Zealand have encountered triumphs in reviving their social character and getting legitimate acknowledgment of their freedoms. The Deal of Waitangi, endorsed in 1840 between the English Crown and Maori bosses, shapes the reason for Maori land freedoms and social safeguarding. The Waitangi Council, laid out in 1975, gives a system to tending to verifiable complaints and guaranteeing the continuous security of Maori freedoms.

Canada's way to deal with compromise with its Native people groups includes recognizing verifiable wrongs, tending to the effect of private schools, and pursuing significant associations. Reality and Compromise Commission of Canada has been instrumental in reporting the historical backdrop of private schools, giving a stage to survivors to share their encounters, and making suggestions for fundamental change.

The effective execution of common freedoms standards frequently requires a complex methodology that consolidates legitimate structures, grassroots activism, and worldwide coordinated effort. Endeavors to battle illegal exploitation and present day bondage, for instance, have seen improvement through a mix of lawful measures, mindfulness missions, and participation among legislatures and non-administrative associations.

The Unified Countries Manageable Improvement Objectives (SDGs) address a complete system that incorporates basic freedoms standards into worldwide endeavors to address squeezing difficulties, including destitution, disparity, and natural manageability. The SDGs perceive the interconnectedness of different basic liberties issues and highlight the requirement for all encompassing methodologies that abandon nobody.

The job of innovation in propelling common liberties is progressively critical. Computerized devices and stages give roads to backing, activation, and documentation of denials of basic liberties. Web-based entertainment, specifically, plays had a pivotal impact in enhancing minimized voices, bringing issues to light of common freedoms infringement, and cultivating worldwide fortitude.

Notwithstanding, the computerized domain likewise presents difficulties, like the potential for reconnaissance, online provocation, and the spread of disinformation. Effective executions of common freedoms standards in the advanced age require cautious thought of the moral elements of innovation, the security of online protection, and endeavors to connect the computerized partition.

Challenges endure in the worldwide acknowledgment of basic freedoms. Tyrant systems, furnished clashes, monetary disparity, and fundamental segregation present considerable snags. The ascent of libertarian developments in different regions of the planet challenges the comprehensiveness of basic freedoms and highlights the significance of continuous support and schooling to balance troublesome stories.

All in all, looking at effective executions of basic liberties standards uncovers both the potential for positive change and the continuous difficulties in accomplishing a reality where common freedoms are generally regarded and secured. LGBTQ+ freedoms headways, momentary equity processes, inability privileges, orientation uniformity strategies, native privileges acknowledgment, and endeavors towards compromise all show that progress is conceivable through coordinated endeavors at different levels.

These examples of overcoming adversity highlight the significance of an all encompassing and multifaceted way to deal with basic freedoms, perceiving the interconnectedness of various issues. They feature the job of people, networks, common society, and the worldwide local area in propelling basic freedoms standards. As the world keeps on wrestling with complex difficulties, the examples gained from fruitful executions can direct future endeavors towards an all the more, comprehensive, and privileges regarding worldwide society.

5.2 Highlighting positive change and progress

Positive change and progress are vital parts of human turn of events, mirroring the limit of people, networks, and social orders to defeat difficulties and take a stab at progress. In different domains, from civil rights to mechanical advancement, examples of positive change act as encouraging signs, representing the extraordinary force of aggregate endeavors and visionary drives.

One outstanding region where positive change has been apparent is the worldwide decrease in outrageous destitution. Throughout recent many years, deliberate endeavors by legislatures, non-administrative associations (NGOs), and worldwide establishments have added to lifting a huge number of individuals out of outrageous destitution. The Unified Countries' Thousand years Improvement Objectives (MDGs) and, later, the Maintainable Improvement Objectives (SDGs) set aggressive focuses to address destitution, craving, and imbalance, cultivating a worldwide obligation to positive change.

China's exceptional monetary change remains as a paradigmatic illustration of how supported endeavors can prompt positive change for a gigantic scope. Throughout recent many years, China has lifted a huge number of individuals out of destitution through financial changes, framework improvement, and designated neediness mitigation programs. The outcome of China's destitution decrease drives shows the potential for vital preparation and far reaching strategies to achieve groundbreaking change.

In the domain of medical services, critical headway has been made in the battle against irresistible sicknesses. The worldwide reaction to illnesses like HIV/Helps, jungle fever, and tuberculosis has prompted better counteraction, treatment, and mindfulness. Drives like the Worldwide Asset to Battle Helps, Tuberculosis and Jungle fever play had a urgent impact in preparing assets and planning endeavors to battle these illnesses on a worldwide scale.

Positive change is likewise apparent in the rising admittance to schooling around the world. Endeavors to accomplish widespread essential schooling, as framed in the MDGs and further underscored in the SDGs, have added to critical headways. Numerous nations have gained ground in extending instructive open doors, decreasing orientation abberations, and upgrading the nature of training. The acknowledgment of schooling as a central basic freedom highlights its significance in encouraging individual strengthening and cultural advancement.

Ladies' privileges and orientation uniformity have seen positive changes, but with continuous difficulties. The worldwide ladies' freedoms development has been instrumental in getting lawful changes, testing unfair practices, and advancing ladies' support in different circles. The Me Too development, for example, has catalyzed discussions around inappropriate behavior, enhancing the voices of survivors and requesting responsibility.

Rwanda's post-destruction venture remembers critical advancement for ladies' portrayal in legislative issues. Following the staggering destruction in 1994, which lopsidedly impacted ladies, Rwanda has arisen as a worldwide forerunner concerning ladies' political portrayal. Portions and governmental policy regarding minorities in society measures have brought about a huge level of ladies holding seats in Rwanda's parliament, showing the way that deliberate strategies can achieve positive change in orientation elements.

Natural protection endeavors address a basic space where positive change is basic for the prosperity of the planet. The worldwide acknowledgment of environmental change as a major problem has prompted expanded mindfulness, strategy measures, and global collaboration. Drives like the Paris Arrangement mean to restrict worldwide temperature increments and alleviate the effect of environmental change, accentuating the requirement for aggregate activity to defend the climate.

Environmentally friendly power progressions offer an encouraging sign in the change to additional supportable practices. The rising reception of sun powered, wind, and other sustainable power sources reflects positive change in the mission for spotless and manageable other options. Mechanical developments and interests in environmentally friendly power foundation add to decreasing fossil fuel byproducts and tending to the difficulties presented by environmental change.

The advanced unrest has introduced extraordinary changes across different areas, improving network, correspondence, and admittance to data. The positive effect of innovation is apparent in fields like medical services, schooling, and financial strengthening. Versatile wellbeing applications, online schooling stages, and advanced monetary administrations can possibly span holes and work on the personal satisfaction for millions all over the planet.

Online entertainment stages have become amazing assets for activism and backing, intensifying minimized voices and encouraging worldwide discussions. Developments like People of color Matter, which started in light of racial foul play, have picked up speed through web-based entertainment, prompting expanded mindfulness, strategy conversations, and calls for foundational change. The democratization of data through advanced stages adds to positive change by working with public talk and preparing networks for civil rights.

The worldwide reaction to the Coronavirus pandemic is a new illustration of cooperative endeavors and logical progressions prompting positive change. The quick turn of events and conveyance of antibodies, global participation in sharing assets and information, and the flexibility of medical care frameworks highlight humankind's capacity to answer aggregately to exceptional difficulties. The pandemic has featured the significance of worldwide fortitude and the requirement for facilitated endeavors to resolve complex worldwide issues.

In the domain of common liberties, positive changes are obvious in the developing acknowledgment of LGBTQ+ freedoms. Numerous nations have decriminalized same-sex connections, authorized enemy of separation regulations, and legitimized same-sex marriage. The change in cultural mentalities towards more prominent acknowledgment and inclusivity reflects positive change in the comprehension of basic liberties and the nobility, everything being equal, no matter what their sexual direction or orientation personality.

Native privileges backing has additionally seen positive changes, with expanded acknowledgment of the freedoms of native people groups to their properties, societies, and self-assurance. Lawful structures, like the Unified Countries Statement on the Freedoms of Native People groups, give an establishment to positive change by recognizing and safeguarding the privileges of native networks around the world.

The job of youth in driving positive change has become progressively articulated. Youth-drove developments, for example, Fridays for Future started by Greta Thunberg, have assembled millions around the world to request atrocity on environmental change. Youthful activists are supporting civil rights purposes, pushing for basic freedoms, and testing foundational imbalances, showing the capability of youth commitment in molding an additional fair and feasible future.

The progress of microfinance drives in enabling business people in non-industrial nations shows how designated mediations can prompt positive change at the grassroots level. Microfinance gives little advances and monetary administrations to people in underserved networks, empowering them to begin or extend private ventures. This approach has a gradually expanding influence, adding to neediness decrease, ladies' strengthening, and local area improvement.

In post-struggle settings, peacebuilding and compromise endeavors address pathways to positive change. Drives that connect with networks in discourse, address the underlying drivers of contention, and elevate social attachment add to revamping social orders destroyed by savagery. The job of truth and compromise commissions, as found in South Africa and different settings, shows the potential for positive change through recognizing past wrongs and encouraging recuperating.

Training for manageable improvement embodies the reconciliation of positive change into educational programs to develop a feeling of obligation and ecological stewardship among people in the future. By consolidating standards of supportability, morals, and worldwide citizenship into training, social orders can encourage an outlook that values social and ecological prosperity. Schooling turns into an instrument for imparting values and information that add to positive change.

Taking everything into account, featuring positive change and progress across different areas highlights the strength and versatility of people and social orders. From destitution decrease and headways in medical care to orientation correspondence, natural protection, and mechanical development, cases of positive change offer motivation and examples for what's to come. The aggregate endeavors of networks, states, activists, and global joint efforts add to building an all the more, fair, and economical world. As the worldwide local area faces continuous difficulties, the tales of positive change act as encouraging signs, helping us to remember the extraordinary force of human organization and aggregate activity.

5.3 Role of international organizations and grassroots movements

The job of worldwide associations and grassroots developments in forming worldwide elements, encouraging collaboration, and it is urgent in the contemporary world to address complex difficulties. These substances work at various levels, yet their exchange frequently brings about a synergistic way to deal with propelling common liberties, advancing manageable turn of events, and resolving worldwide issues. Analyzing the complex connection between worldwide associations and grassroots developments gives bits of knowledge into how these different entertainers add to positive shift and impact the direction of worldwide undertakings.

Worldwide associations, enveloping substances like the Unified Countries (UN), the World Wellbeing Association (WHO), and the Worldwide Financial Asset (IMF), assume a focal part in encouraging worldwide collaboration and tending to transnational difficulties. These associations act as discussions for strategic talks, stages for shared direction, and instruments for organizing endeavors on issues that rise above public lines.

The Unified Countries, laid out in the repercussions of The Second Great War, stays a foundation of worldwide participation. The UN Contract frames standards of sovereign balance, non-impedance in homegrown issues, and the serene goal of contentions. Its particular organizations, including the UNICEF, UNDP, and UNHCR, center around unambiguous parts of worldwide difficulties, like youngsters' privileges, improvement, and exiles, individually.

Global associations work with cooperation on basic issues like environmental change, general wellbeing emergencies, and demilitarization. The Paris Arrangement, haggled under the sponsorship of the UN System Show on Environmental Change (UNFCCC), embodies worldwide endeavors to address environmental change through responsibilities to decrease ozone depleting substance discharges.

Likewise, the WHO assumes a urgent part in planning reactions to pandemics, as shown during the Coronavirus pandemic, where it gave direction, worked with data sharing, and upheld immunization circulation endeavors.

The IMF and World Bank, while confronting scrutinizes for their effect on monetary arrangements, act as central members in global monetary participation. They give monetary help, strategy guidance, and specialized mastery to part nations, expecting to advance financial strength and improvement. The worldwide monetary engineering, molded by these foundations, has suggestions for the financial prosperity of countries and highlights the interconnectedness of the worldwide economy.

Grassroots developments, then again, exude from nearby networks and people pushing for explicit causes, frequently established in civil rights, basic liberties, and ecological worries. These developments tackle the force of aggregate activity to impact change, testing laid out standards, and requesting responsibility from states and foundations. Grassroots activism is described by its decentralized nature, variety of members, and granular perspective.

The People of color Matter development, which acquired conspicuousness in the US and extended universally, represents the groundbreaking effect of grassroots activism. Ignited by occurrences of police fierceness against Dark people, the development advocates for a finish to foundational bigotry, police savagery, and racial shamefulness. Grassroots preparation, frequently worked with through web-based entertainment, has prompted far reaching fights, strategy conversations, and expanded consciousness of racial disparity.

Natural developments, for example, Fridays for Future drove by Greta Thunberg, feature the job of youth-drove activism in tending to environmental change. The development, started by a solitary person's school strike for environment activity, has advanced into a worldwide peculiarity with a large number of youngsters taking part in strikes and pushing for pressing environment activity. Grassroots ecological activism accentuates the significance of individual organization in driving foundational change.

The Me Too development, beginning from grassroots endeavors to bring issues to light about inappropriate behavior and attack, represents how online entertainment can intensify minimized voices and catalyze worldwide discussions. What started as a hashtag via web-based entertainment stages developed into a more extensive development, inciting conversations on power elements, assent, and responsibility. Grassroots drives, driven by survivors and activists, have added to changes parents in law, work environment strategies, and cultural mentalities towards sexual offense.

In the domain of native privileges, grassroots developments have been instrumental in pushing for the acknowledgment of native people groups' property freedoms, social conservation, and self-assurance.

Developments like Inactive Not any more in Canada and fights against the Dakota Access Pipeline in the US feature the flexibility of native networks in affirming their freedoms and testing strategies that undermine their prosperity.

The cooperative energy between global associations and grassroots developments is clear in their cooperative endeavors to propel shared objectives. Common society associations, frequently established in grassroots activism, draw in with global discussions to impact strategy choices, consider legislatures responsible, and add to the execution of peaceful accords. This cooperation reinforces the connection between worldwide administration structures and the different voices and points of view of nearby networks.

Basic liberties support gives a ripe ground to the crossing point of global associations and grassroots developments. The Widespread Statement of Basic liberties, embraced by the UN General Gathering in 1948, fills in as a central report that frames the inborn poise and equivalent privileges, everything being equal. Worldwide associations, including the UN Basic freedoms Board, assume a critical part in observing common liberties infringement, advancing responsibility, and setting worldwide principles.

Grassroots common freedoms developments, frequently powered by the encounters of minimized networks, add to molding the basic liberties plan. Developments pushing for LGBTQ+ freedoms, ladies' privileges, and racial equity feature the diversity of common liberties issues and underline the significance of tending to fundamental imbalances. Worldwide associations, thusly, give stages to these developments to share their encounters, add to strategy conversations, and consider states responsible for common freedoms infringement.

The Show on the Disposal of All Types of Oppression Ladies (CEDAW), took on by the UN General Gathering in 1979, represents the crossing point of global endeavors and grassroots activism in propelling orientation correspondence. CEDAW lays out the privileges of ladies and young ladies and requires the disposal of segregation in light of orientation. Grassroots ladies' developments, for example, the worldwide women's activist development and nearby associations upholding for ladies' freedoms, add to the execution of CEDAW standards at the grassroots level.

The job of worldwide associations and grassroots developments is especially articulated in struggle and post-struggle circumstances. The Unified Countries Security Gathering, liable for keeping up with global harmony and security, frequently teams up with grassroots peacebuilding drives to address the underlying drivers of contention and advance compromise. Nearby peacebuilders assume a basic part in cultivating discourse, building trust, and pushing for maintainable harmony.

Truth and compromise commissions, laid out in the repercussions of contentions, give a space to tending to past barbarities and advancing recuperating. The South African Truth and Compromise Commission, for example, worked with a course of recognizing common liberties infringement, conceding reprieve in return for truth-telling, and establishing the groundwork for a more comprehensive and just society. The cooperation between global standards and neighborhood endeavors is obvious in temporary equity processes around the world.

While global associations and grassroots developments share shared objectives, provokes emerge due to varying points of view, power elements, and asset incongruities.

Worldwide associations, frequently portrayed by regulatory designs and conciliatory contemplations, may confront restrictions in answering quickly to grassroots worries. Grassroots developments, while dynamic and responsive, may experience impediments in getting to worldwide gatherings and affecting dynamic cycles.

The consideration of different voices in global gatherings is vital for successful and impartial administration. Endeavors to upgrade the support of common society, including grassroots associations, in worldwide dynamic cycles are progressing. The Assembled Countries' Plan 2030 for Reasonable Advancement stresses the significance of comprehensive organizations, perceiving that practical improvement requires cooperation between states, common society, and the confidential area.

Worldwide developments for civil rights, like the World Social Discussion, give spaces to discourse and joint effort between global associations and grassroots developments. These gatherings work with trades of thoughts, procedures, and encounters, cultivating a more comprehensive way to deal with tending to worldwide difficulties. The enunciation of shared values, like civil rights, common liberties, and ecological manageability, turns into an extension between the nearby and the worldwide.

The Feasible Improvement Objectives (SDGs), took on by the UN in 2015, embody an extensive system that coordinates global yearnings with grassroots worries. The SDGs address issues, for example, destitution, disparity, environment activity, and harmony, perceiving the interconnectedness of worldwide difficulties. Grassroots associations add to the SDGs by carrying out projects at the nearby level, upholding for strategy changes.

Grassroots developments encapsulate the force of conventional individuals meeting up to address social, political, and ecological issues at the neighborhood level. These developments, frequently beginning starting from the earliest stage inside networks, are described by their decentralized construction, aggregate navigation, and obligation to affecting change through direct activity. Looking at the nature, effect, and meaning of grassroots developments gives significant bits of knowledge into their job as impetuses for social change and promoters for equity.

At the center of grassroots developments is a pledge to resolving issues that straightforwardly influence neighborhood networks. Whether it is supporting for ecological preservation, testing fundamental imbalances, or advancing basic liberties, these developments are driven by a need to get moving and an acknowledgment that change is essential for the prosperity of people and networks. The issues they tackle are in many cases well established in neighborhood settings, and grassroots developments act as systems for communicating the worries and desires of those straightforwardly impacted.

Natural grassroots developments assume a urgent part in bringing issues to light about biological issues and pushing for feasible practices. The natural development has a rich history, with achievements like the Chipko development in India, where nearby networks embraced peaceful direct activity to safeguard trees from logging. All the more as of late, the Annihilation Defiance development has acquired worldwide consideration for its calls to address the environment emergency through common rebellion and promotion for intense strategy changes.

The battle against racial treachery has been a focal point of grassroots developments since forever ago. The social liberties development in the US during the 1950s and 1960s is a turning point in the battle for racial fairness. Driven by figures like Martin Luther Lord Jr., the development utilized peaceful opposition and grassroots getting sorted out to challenge isolation and prejudicial regulations. Contemporary developments like People of color Matter proceed with this inheritance, tending to foundational prejudice, police savagery, and upholding for social and lawful changes.

Ladies' privileges developments, established in grassroots activism, have been instrumental in testing orientation based segregation and pushing for equivalent freedoms. The suffragette development in the mid twentieth century battled for ladies' more right than wrong to cast a ballot, making way for more extensive orientation equity endeavors. The women's activist development, enveloping influxes of activism, keeps on resolving issues like conceptive freedoms, working environment segregation, and savagery against ladies.

Grassroots developments in the domain of LGBTQ+ privileges have been essential in testing cultural standards and pushing for equivalent freedoms and acknowledgment. Pride developments, rising up out of the battle for LGBTQ+ privileges, praise variety and request a finish to segregation in light of sexual direction or orientation character. Grassroots activism inside the LGBTQ+ people group has added to legitimate progressions, like the decriminalization of homosexuality and the acknowledgment of same-sex marriage in different nations.

Native privileges developments are much of the time attached in grassroots endeavors to safeguard genealogical terrains, protect social legacy, and affirm self-assurance. Developments like Standing Stone in the US, which went against the development of the Dakota Access

Pipeline through consecrated native terrains, feature the crossing point of ecological and native freedoms activism. These developments stress the significance of perceiving and regarding the freedoms and independence of native networks.

Grassroots developments likewise assume a basic part in tending to financial imbalances and supporting for laborers' freedoms. Work developments, generally established in grassroots getting sorted out, have battled for fair wages, safe working circumstances, and the right to aggregate haggling. Developments like the Battle for $15 in the US look to raise the lowest pay permitted by law, tending to monetary variations and pushing for the prosperity of low-wage laborers.

Common liberties developments, enveloping a scope of issues from opportunity of articulation to one side to training, frequently track down their foundations in grassroots activism. Acquittal Worldwide, established by people supporting for the arrival of political detainees, embodies the effect of grassroots endeavors in the basic liberties field. Grassroots associations and developments add to recording denials of basic liberties, offering help to casualties, and upholding for lawful and strategy changes.

The force of innovation has enhanced the effect of grassroots developments, giving stages to arranging, assembling backing, and bringing issues to light. Web-based entertainment, specifically, has turned into an incredible asset for grassroots activists to interface with a worldwide crowd. Developments like the Middle Easterner Spring, which used web-based entertainment stages to arrange fights and offer data, epitomize the groundbreaking capability of computerized apparatuses in grassroots activism.

Grassroots developments frequently work even with difficulties, including restraint, resistance, and asset imperatives. Dictator systems might try to stifle grassroots activism, seeing it as a danger to their position. The crackdown on favorable to a majority rules government activists in different regions of the planet features the dangers that grassroots coordinators face in supporting for political change. In spite of these difficulties, grassroots developments continue, exhibiting flexibility and versatility even with difficulty.

The decentralized idea of grassroots developments takes into consideration more prominent inclusivity and variety of voices. Not at all like various leveled structures, grassroots getting sorted out frequently includes a huge number of members, each contributing remarkable points of view and encounters. This inclusivity is a strength, as it guarantees that an expansive scope of worries and perspectives are addressed, prompting more exhaustive and nuanced ways to deal with social issues.

The outcome of grassroots developments is many times estimated by quick approach changes as well as by their capacity to move cultural perspectives and standards.

Developments testing social practices, prejudicial convictions, or severe frameworks may not accomplish prompt legitimate triumphs but rather can add to a more extensive social shift. The LGBTQ+ privileges development, for instance, plays had a significant impact in changing cultural mentalities towards sexual direction and orientation personality.

The effect of grassroots developments stretches out past authoritative changes to impacting constituent legislative issues. Developments that activate citizens, bring issues to light, and backer for explicit strategy positions add to molding political plans. Grassroots activism can consider lawmakers responsible, impact party stages, and effect the results of decisions. The Casual get-together development in the US and its impact on moderate legislative issues is an illustration of grassroots activism molding political talk.

Worldwide associations frequently assume a correlative part in supporting and enhancing the endeavors of grassroots developments. Basic freedoms associations, for example, work together with neighborhood activists, give assets, and intensify their voices on the worldwide stage. The Unified Countries and its different offices act as stages for grassroots associations to share their encounters, add to strategy conversations, and consider states responsible for basic liberties infringement.

The transaction between grassroots developments and worldwide associations is apparent in worldwide missions resolving issues like destitution, schooling, and general wellbeing. Crusades like the Worldwide Training Development, supporting for expanded admittance to schooling around the world, benefit from coordinated effort between grassroots associations, global NGOs, and administrative bodies. Grassroots drives give on-the-ground bits of knowledge, while worldwide associations contribute assets, aptitude, and worldwide reach.

Cooperation between worldwide associations and grassroots developments is especially articulated in tending to worldwide difficulties that rise above public boundaries. Environmental change, for instance, requires composed endeavors at the nearby, public, and worldwide levels. Grassroots ecological developments, upholding for economical practices and testing destructive arrangements, add to the more extensive worldwide talk on environment activity. Worldwide associations give systems to exchanges, coordinate assets, and work with information dividing between countries.

The Unified Countries Manageable Improvement Objectives (SDGs) epitomize a worldwide plan that tries to address interconnected difficulties through cooperation between states, global associations, and grassroots endeavors. Grassroots associations add to the accomplishment of explicit SDGs by carrying out projects, bringing issues to light, and supporting for strategy changes at the neighborhood level. The SDGs feature the significance of comprehensive associations to accomplish supportable turn of events.

Grassroots developments add to the democratization of dynamic cycles by giving an offset to hierarchical methodologies. The contribution of neighborhood networks in navigation guarantees that strategies and drives are educated by the real factors and needs regarding those straightforwardly impacted. Participatory methodologies, as found in local area drove improvement projects, engage people and networks to shape their own fates.

Notwithstanding, pressures can emerge between grassroots developments and worldwide associations. Worries about co-optation, where the objectives of grassroots developments are weakened or diverted to fit outer plans, are legitimate. Grassroots activists might oppose lining up with worldwide associations on the off chance that they see an absence of veritable coordinated effort or on the other hand in the event that the global elements are viewed as segregated from nearby real factors.

Chapter 6

Human Rights and Social Justice

Common freedoms and civil rights are basic rules that support the texture of a fair and impartial society. These ideas have developed over hundreds of years, molded by social, philosophical, and lawful structures, mirroring the aggregate yearnings of mankind for an existence where each individual is treated with nobility, regard, and reasonableness.

At the core of the talk on common freedoms is the acknowledgment of the innate worth and equivalent privileges of every individual, no matter what their experience, personality, or conditions. The possibility that specific privileges are widespread and natural has built up some forward movement around the world, tracking down articulation in different global reports, like the Widespread Statement of Common liberties (UDHR), took on by the Unified Countries General Gathering in 1948.

The UDHR addresses a milestone throughout the entire existence of common liberties, articulating a dream of a reality where everybody appreciates opportunity, equity, and harmony. It incorporates a wide range of freedoms, including common, political, monetary, social, and social privileges. These freedoms are interrelated and indissoluble, shaping an exhaustive system that tries to address the complex elements of human life.

Common and political privileges, like the right to life, freedom, and a fair preliminary, establish the groundwork for individual independence and insurance against inconsistent state activities. These privileges are fundamental for encouraging a vote based society where residents can take part in administration and consider specialists responsible. Then again, monetary, social, and social freedoms, for example, the option to work, schooling, and wellbeing, are vital to guaranteeing a good way of life and advancing civil rights.

Civil rights, an idea firmly interlaced with basic liberties, underscores the fair conveyance of assets, potential open doors, and honors inside a general public. It calls for tending to fundamental imbalances and separation, destroying boundaries that ruin equivalent investment, and encouraging inclusivity. Accomplishing civil rights requires lawful and strategy measures as well as a change of cultural mentalities and designs that sustain unfairness.

Nonetheless, the acknowledgment of common freedoms and civil rights faces various difficulties. Imbalances continue across the globe, with underestimated networks frequently encountering segregation in view of elements like race, orientation, identity, religion, and financial status. Tending to these incongruities requires a comprehensive methodology that consolidates legitimate components, social strategies, and social movements.

The legitimate structure for basic freedoms is laid out through worldwide settlements, territorial shows, and public regulations. These instruments give a premise to considering states responsible for common freedoms infringement and engage people to look for change. Be that as it may, the adequacy of lawful instruments relies upon their authorization and execution, which shifts generally across various locales.

Also, the understanding and use of basic liberties standards are dependent upon social and logical contemplations. Social relativism, the possibility that basic liberties ought to be grasped inside the setting of each culture's qualities and customs, has been a disputed matter. Finding some kind of harmony between regarding social variety and maintaining widespread common freedoms norms represents an intricate test for the worldwide local area.

Civil rights, as an idea established in moral and moral standards, reaches out past legitimate systems. It includes reshaping cultural perspectives and designs to encourage inclusivity and equivalent open doors.

Training assumes an essential part in this cycle, as it shapes people's viewpoints and values. Endeavors to advance civil rights frequently include testing generalizations, advancing variety and consideration, and encouraging compassion and understanding.

The multifacetedness of common liberties and civil rights is especially obvious in the battles of underestimated gatherings. Ladies, for example, have for quite some time been at the very front of developments pushing for orientation uniformity and the acknowledgment of ladies' freedoms as common liberties. The women's activist development has tested settled in male centric standards, calling for equivalent open doors, conceptive privileges, and a finish to orientation based brutality.

Likewise, racial and ethnic minorities have assembled against fundamental bigotry and separation. Developments like the social equality development in the US, against politically-sanctioned racial segregation battles in South Africa, and Native privileges developments overall have looked to destroy structures that sustain racial shamefulness and guarantee the full acknowledgment of the freedoms of minority networks.

The LGBTQ+ privileges development has likewise been a huge power in propelling basic freedoms and civil rights. The battle for equivalent privileges, acknowledgment, and security against segregation in view of sexual direction and orientation personality has picked up speed all around the world. Endeavors to decriminalize homosexuality, perceive same-sex connections, and battle viciousness against LGBTQ+ people mirror the continuous battle for a more comprehensive and just society.

In the domain of monetary and social freedoms, the worldwide local area wrestles with issues of destitution, disparity, and admittance to fundamental necessities. The right to schooling, for instance, stays slippery for some because of monetary hindrances, orientation inclinations, and lacking framework. Guaranteeing all inclusive admittance to quality training isn't just a question of common freedoms yet additionally a vital driver of social advancement and monetary turn of events.

Wellbeing, as a major part of human prosperity, is complicatedly connected to civil rights. Abberations in medical services access, exacerbated by elements, for example, pay disparity and foundational separation, feature the requirement for wellbeing frameworks that focus on value. The Coronavirus pandemic has highlighted the significance of a planned worldwide reaction to wellbeing emergencies and the need to guarantee that immunizations and clinical assets are dispersed reasonably.

Ecological equity is an arising aspect of both basic freedoms and civil rights. The effect of natural debasement and environmental change lopsidedly influences weak networks, frequently worsening existing imbalances. The right to a solid climate and practical improvement are progressively perceived as fundamental parts of the more extensive common liberties system.

Notwithstanding the headway made in propelling basic freedoms and civil rights, the world keeps on wrestling with determined difficulties. Dictator systems and egalitarian developments in different pieces of the globe present dangers to law and order, majority rule foundations, and individual opportunities. The ascent of patriotism and xenophobia further mixtures endeavors to make an additional comprehensive and open minded world.

Moreover, the fast speed of mechanical headway brings up moral issues about security, reconnaissance, and the effect of computerized reasoning on common liberties. The advanced gap intensifies existing disparities, restricting admittance to data and open doors for those without satisfactory mechanical assets. Offsetting mechanical development with moral contemplations is a squeezing worry for the worldwide local area.

Tending to these difficulties requires an aggregate and multi-faceted methodology. Worldwide collaboration, exchange, and discretion assume urgent parts in cultivating a common obligation to basic liberties and civil rights. Discretionary endeavors, like basic freedoms discoursed and global meetings, give stages to states to participate in useful conversations and trade best practices.

Non-legislative associations (NGOs) and common society assume an essential part in considering states responsible and supporting for the freedoms of minimized networks. Basic liberties protectors frequently face dangers and oppression for their work, featuring the significance of shielding the space for common society to openly work. Support for grassroots developments and activism is fundamental for driving social change.

Schooling stays a foundation for imparting upsides of common freedoms and civil rights. Coordinating common liberties instruction into school educational plans and advancing mindfulness through different channels add to making a culture of regard for variety and incorporation. Instructive organizations likewise assume a part in encouraging decisive reasoning and engaging people to challenge treachery.

Organizations and companies are progressively perceiving their obligation to regard basic freedoms. Corporate social obligation (CSR) drives, moral strategic approaches, and production network straightforwardness add to advancing fair work rehearses and ecological supportability. The business area's commitment to maintaining common liberties mirrors a developing consciousness of the interconnectedness between financial exercises and social prosperity.

The job of media in molding general assessment and viewing ability to be answerable couldn't possibly be more significant. A free and free media is fundamental for scattering data, uncovering denials of basic liberties, and encouraging public talk. Media proficiency projects and drives to battle falsehood add to making an educated and drew in populace.

Worldwide foundations, like the Unified Countries and local bodies, assume a focal part in setting common liberties guidelines and organizing endeavors to address worldwide difficulties. The UN Common freedoms Chamber, for instance, conducts normal surveys of states' basic liberties records and works with discourse on major problems. The Global Crook Court tries to consider people responsible for intolerable basic freedoms infringement.

At the public level, established securities, free legal authorities, and powerful lawful structures are fundamental for maintaining common liberties. Public common liberties organizations and ombudsman workplaces act as me.

6.1 Linking human rights to broader social justice issues

Connecting basic liberties to more extensive civil rights issues is fundamental for making a thorough system that tends to the intricacies of cultural disparities. While basic freedoms center around the intrinsic nobility and equity, all things considered, civil rights stretches out this viewpoint to consider the primary, fundamental, and social factors that add to incongruities among different gatherings. Understanding the interconnectedness of basic freedoms and civil rights is vital for creating procedures that advance a fair and comprehensive society.

At its center, the idea of common liberties includes the basic thought that each individual is qualified for specific privileges and opportunities just by righteousness of being human. These freedoms incorporate common and political freedoms, financial and social privileges, and social and natural contemplations. The General Statement of Common freedoms (UDHR), took on by the Unified Countries in 1948, fills in as a fundamental record illustrating these standards. In any case, perceiving basic liberties alone is deficient without tending to the more extensive social setting that shapes the conveyance of these privileges.

Civil rights goes past lawful and institutional systems, diving into the underlying drivers of disparity and treachery. It looks to recognize and destroy boundaries that obstruct equivalent open doors and fair treatment. By connecting common freedoms to civil rights, a more all encompassing methodology arises — one that recognizes the interaction between individual privileges and the more extensive cultural designs that either work with or impede the acknowledgment of those freedoms.

One basic part of connecting common liberties to civil rights is figuring out the effect of monetary differences on the delight in key freedoms. Monetary disparity can restrict admittance to instruction, medical services, lodging, and work potential open doors, making a pattern of impediment that lopsidedly influences minimized networks. In this way, endeavors to advance basic liberties should address financial shameful acts and supporter for arrangements that cultivate impartial dispersion of assets.

Training, as a major basic freedom, fills in as an illustrative illustration of the crossing point between individual privileges and civil rights. While the right to schooling is cherished in different global deals, social and financial factors frequently make boundaries to instructive access. Financial status, orientation, nationality, and geological area can impact one's capacity to get quality schooling. By tending to these civil rights issues, for example, financial disparity and foundational separation, the full acknowledgment of the right to training turns out to be more achievable.

Essentially, the right to wellbeing is unpredictably connected to more extensive civil rights concerns. Admittance to medical care administrations, clean conditions, and sufficient nourishment are fundamental parts of the right to wellbeing. Nonetheless, foundational issues like destitution, segregation, and ecological corruption can sabotage people's capacity to completely partake in this right. Connecting wellbeing related basic freedoms to civil rights includes tending to social determinants of wellbeing, pushing for medical care value, and encouraging arrangements that focus on general wellbeing over benefit thought processes.

With regards to civil rights, issues of racial and ethnic disparity are diligent difficulties that cross with common liberties concerns. Segregation, foundational bigotry, and racial variations in admittance to assets and open doors block the acknowledgment of common liberties for underestimated networks. The battle for racial equity is, subsequently, an indispensable piece of the more extensive common liberties development. Perceiving and destroying racial bad form contributes not exclusively to the particular privileges of impacted people yet in addition to the general advancement of common freedoms standards.

Moreover, the freedoms of ladies are indivisible from civil rights contemplations. Orientation based separation, viciousness, and inconsistent admittance to open doors are inescapable issues that cross with more extensive cultural standards and power structures. The women's activist development, established chasing after orientation uniformity, advocates for the acknowledgment of ladies' privileges as basic freedoms. By tending to orientation based social treacheries, progress toward the satisfaction of ladies' common liberties is progressed, advancing a more comprehensive and impartial society.

Sexual direction and orientation personality address another aspect where basic freedoms and civil rights converge. LGBTQ+ people frequently face separation, savagery, and legitimate difficulties in view of their sexual direction or orientation character. The battle for LGBTQ+ freedoms is a battle against cultural biases and fundamental treacheries, connecting basic liberties standards with the more extensive journey for civil rights and inclusivity.

The freedoms of native people groups additionally epitomize the interconnectedness of common liberties and civil rights. Native people group frequently face verifiable treacheries, land dispossession, and social minimization.

Perceiving and regarding the freedoms of native people groups includes tending to the verifiable and continuous social treacheries they experience, encouraging social protection, and guaranteeing their full support in choices that influence them.

Natural equity is an arising region where basic freedoms cross with more extensive social and environmental worries. The right to a sound climate is progressively perceived as vital to the general system of basic freedoms. Natural debasement, environmental change, and unreasonable asset abuse lopsidedly influence underestimated networks, connecting ecological equity with civil rights. Endeavors to resolve these issues include supporting for maintainable turn of events, relieving the effect of environmental change, and guaranteeing that natural strategies focus on the prosperity, everything being equal.

In connecting common liberties to civil rights, the idea of diversity becomes critical. Interconnection perceives that people might encounter covering types of segregation in view of different meeting factors, like race, orientation, class, sexual direction, and handicap. Understanding the intricacy of people's characters and the converging idea of separation is fundamental for creating comprehensive and powerful procedures that address the assorted difficulties individuals face in the public eye.

One of the vital difficulties chasing common liberties and civil rights is the presence of foundational structures that propagate disparity. These designs can appear in different structures, including systematized segregation, inconsistent conveyance of assets, and one-sided general sets of laws. Tending to fundamental treacheries requires an exhaustive methodology that goes past individual freedoms infringement to look at and correct the basic designs that propagate disparity.

Lawful structures assume a vital part in connecting common freedoms to civil rights. While basic freedoms regulations give an establishment to safeguarding individual freedoms, civil rights contemplations require legitimate measures that address foundational disparities. Hostile to segregation regulations, governmental policy regarding minorities in society approaches, and measures to advance equivalent open doors are instances of lawful apparatuses pointed toward correcting verifiable and primary shameful acts. Nonetheless, the adequacy of these regulations relies upon their requirement and the responsibility of society to maintain the standards of civil rights.

Common society and non-legislative associations (NGOs) assume a crucial part in connecting basic freedoms to more extensive civil rights issues. Promotion bunches frequently overcome any issues between individual privileges infringement and foundational treacheries by tending to main drivers and preparing public help. Grassroots developments, drove by common society, have been instrumental in testing harsh systems, advancing social change, and propelling the reason for basic liberties and civil rights.

Moreover, the media's job is significant in forming popular assessment and impacting cultural perspectives toward common liberties and civil rights. Dependable reporting can reveal insight into denials of basic liberties, enhance the voices of minimized networks, and consider people with significant influence responsible. Media education and moral revealing add to making an educated populace that is better prepared to comprehend the intricacies of civil rights issues.

The financial components of civil rights are obvious in conversations about abundance disparity, work freedoms, and fair monetary approaches. Financial equity includes inspecting the circulation of assets, potential open doors, and abundance inside a general public. Approaches that advance fair wages, laborers' freedoms, and social wellbeing nets add to monetary equity, lining up with the more extensive objectives of basic liberties and civil rights.

Political support and portrayal are basic parts of both common liberties and civil rights. Comprehensive administration structures that mirror the variety of society add to an all the more and fair political framework. Guaranteeing that underestimated bunches have a voice in dynamic cycles is significant for tending to foundational treacheries and propelling the standards of common freedoms.

Yet again training arises as a groundbreaking device for connecting basic liberties to civil rights. Instructive foundations can assume a part in testing generalizations, advancing inclusivity, and cultivating decisive pondering social issues. Educational program improvement that consolidates different points of view and narratives adds to making a more educated and sympathetic populace.

Strict and social contemplations additionally converge with conversations of basic freedoms and civil rights. While regarding social variety is fundamental, social relativism ought not be utilized as a legitimization for denials of basic liberties. Finding some kind of harmony between social responsiveness and maintaining all inclusive common liberties standards requires.

6.2 Intersectionality and the recognition of diverse identities

Diversity, an idea established in women's activist idea, has arisen as a strong structure for figuring out the mind boggling transaction of social personalities and the subsequent remarkable types of separation and honor that people might insight. Begat by Kimberlé Crenshaw in the last part of the 1980s, diversity challenges shortsighted, single-pivot ways to deal with civil rights by recognizing that individuals' characters are complex and interconnected. The acknowledgment of assorted personalities from the perspective of interconnection is fundamental for tending to the subtleties of abuse, advancing inclusivity, and propelling civil rights.

At its center, diversity perceives that people hold various social personalities, like race, orientation, class, sexual direction, incapacity, and the sky is the limit from there. As opposed to review these personalities in disengagement, multifacetedness looks at how they meet and commonly shape each other, making one of a kind and frequently intensified encounters of honor or underestimation.

For instance, a Person of color might confront particular difficulties that emerge from the crossing point of her race and orientation, which vary from those accomplished by a white lady or an Individual of color.

This system challenges conventional civil rights standards that will generally zero in on solitary parts of personality. By taking into account the convergences of different characters, interconnection gives a more nuanced comprehension of how power designs and frameworks of mistreatment work. It underlines that social characters are not added substance however intelligent, molding people's encounters in manners that can't be completely gotten a handle on by looking at every personality in detachment.

Race and orientation frequently act as focal tomahawks inside conversations of interconnection. By and large, women's activist developments have confronted analysis for fundamentally addressing the worries of white, working class ladies. Interconnection tends to this impediment by recognizing that ladies of variety face novel difficulties that outcome from the crossing point of both orientation and racial characters. Perceiving the variety of ladies' encounters is crucial to building a more comprehensive women's activist development.

Essentially, conversations of racial equity can profit from a multifaceted methodology. Perceiving how different personalities cross with race, like orientation, class, and sexual direction, assists with enlightening the fluctuated encounters inside racial gatherings. This acknowledgment is especially urgent in tending to foundational bigotry, as the effect of racial segregation is frequently entwined with different types of mistreatment.

The LGBTQ+ freedoms development likewise embraces multifacetedness as it perceives the variety of sexual directions, orientation personalities, and articulations. LGBTQ+ people might encounter segregation diversely founded on their converging personalities. For instance, an eccentric ethnic minority might defy novel difficulties that vary from those looked by a white, cisgender gay person. Recognizing these crossing points is fundamental for making comprehensive arrangements and backing that address the fluctuated needs of the LGBTQ+ people group.

Inability crosses with different personalities inside the structure of interconnection. Crippled people might confront separation in light of their handicap, yet this segregation is frequently compounded by variables like race, orientation, and financial status. The acknowledgment of these crossing points is imperative for creating comprehensive strategies that consider the different encounters of debilitated people and address the obstructions they experience in the public eye.

Financial status is one more key part of diversity. Class meets with different personalities, affecting admittance to schooling, medical services, work open doors, and that's just the beginning.

Low-pay people might confront unmistakable difficulties in light of their group, and these difficulties might be intensified by other converging elements like race, orientation, or handicap. Understanding the convergences of class with different characters is essential for creating powerful procedures to address financial imbalance and advance civil rights.

The work environment is a setting where multifacetedness has critical ramifications. Variety and incorporation endeavors that main spotlight on one component of character, like orientation or race, may ignore the special difficulties looked by people with crossing personalities. Working environment strategies should consider what various personalities meet and mean for encounters of segregation, portrayal, and progression. Inability to do so may sustain disparities and prevent the production of genuinely comprehensive workplaces.

Instruction is another field where diversity assumes a basic part. Schools and colleges are different spaces where understudies bring a scope of personalities and encounters. Perceiving the crossing points of race, orientation, financial status, and different elements is fundamental for establishing comprehensive instructive conditions. Comprehensive educational plans, different staff portrayal, and designated help for understudies with meeting characters add to a more evenhanded instructive experience.

Medical care is one more area where interconnection is of central significance. The medical services needs of people are impacted by a bunch of elements, including race, orientation, financial status, and that's only the tip of the iceberg. For instance, the convergence of orientation and race can influence admittance to regenerative medical services, while the crossing point of financial status and inability might influence the accessibility of specific clinical benefits. A medical services framework that perceives and addresses these convergences is better prepared to give quality and evenhanded consideration.

Lawful and law enforcement frameworks are not safe to the ramifications of interconnection. Racial and orientation predispositions can meet, bringing about differential treatment inside the overall set of laws. For example, People of color might confront one of a kind difficulties in the law enforcement framework that emerge from the crossing point of race and orientation. Tending to these crossing points is fundamental for fighting foundational treacheries and advancing a general set of laws that is fair and unprejudiced.

Media portrayal is an integral asset for molding cultural discernments and mentalities. Diversity challenges media depictions that distort or generalize people in light of a solitary part of their personality. Different and nuanced portrayals that mirror the converging characters of people add to a more exact and comprehensive portrayal of society. Media proficiency that consolidates a comprehension of multifacetedness can assist audiences with basically captivating with portrayals in different types of media.

Political portrayal is one more space where the ramifications of diversity are obvious. Guaranteeing different and agent political administration requires a comprehension of how crossing personalities impact people's encounters and points of view. Political choices and approaches that neglect to consider the crossing points of personality may coincidentally propagate imbalances and underestimation.

Strict and social settings additionally meet with different characters, impacting people's encounters of segregation and having a place. A multifaceted way to deal with strict and social variety perceives that people might confront exceptional difficulties in view of the transaction of their strict or social character with different perspectives like race, orientation, or sexual direction. Advancing strict and social inclusivity requires a comprehension of these crossing points.

The language we use in conversations of character and civil rights matters. Interconnection underscores the significance of utilizing comprehensive and conscious language that recognizes the variety of encounters. Phrasing that perceives the crossing points of character, for example, "LGBTQ+ ethnic minorities" or "debilitated ladies," conveys a more precise and conscious comprehension of people's encounters. Language likewise assumes a part in testing generalizations and advancing a more nuanced talk around personality and civil rights.

The diverse methodology has suggestions for policymaking and activism. Strategies and support that consider the crossing points of personality are bound to be viable in tending to the assorted necessities of people. Activism that perceives and intensifies the voices of those with meeting characters adds to a more comprehensive and multifaceted civil rights development. The consideration of different points of view fortifies both arrangement and promotion endeavors, making more complete and fair arrangements.

Nonetheless, the idea of multifacetedness isn't without its difficulties. A few pundits contend that the system can be excessively perplexing or hard to apply practically speaking. Others express worries that an extreme spotlight on interconnection might prompt a type of "mistreatment Olympics," where people seek acknowledgment of their converging characters. Finding some kind of harmony between perceiving the intricacy of character and keeping away from disruptive contest is a continuous test inside multifaceted talk.

6.3 Addressing systemic inequalities and discrimination

Tending to fundamental disparities and segregation is a complex and basic undertaking that requires a thorough methodology across different areas of society.

Foundational imbalances allude to determined, underlying abberations that influence specific gatherings in light of variables like race, orientation, financial status, and the sky is the limit from there. Segregation, whether unequivocal or implied, sustains and builds up these imbalances. Successfully handling fundamental issues requires a guarantee to destroying imbued predispositions, transforming institutional practices, and encouraging comprehensive strategies across different spaces.

One of the primary moves toward tending to foundational imbalances is recognizing the authentic setting that has added to the current inconsistencies. Authentic shameful acts, like bondage, expansionism, and organized segregation, have left enduring engravings on friendly designs. Understanding the authentic underlying foundations of fundamental imbalances is fundamental for creating informed and designated systems to redress these differences.

Race stays a focal hub around which foundational imbalances spin. Networks of variety frequently face excessively higher paces of neediness, restricted admittance to quality schooling and medical services, and improved probability of experiences with the law enforcement framework. Addressing racial disparities requires a guarantee to destroying underlying bigotry, testing prejudicial practices, and setting out open doors for fair portrayal and interest.

In the domain of training, fundamental imbalances are apparent in variations in admittance to quality tutoring and instructive results. Schools in financially hindered regions frequently need assets, experienced educators, and extracurricular open doors. This sustains a pattern of inconvenience, restricting the instructive possibilities of minimized networks. To address fundamental instructive disparities, there should be a coordinated work to distribute assets all the more evenhandedly, execute comprehensive educational programs, and offer designated help for understudies confronting extra difficulties.

Business rehearses contribute essentially to foundational disparities. Separation in recruiting, pay holes, and restricted open doors for professional success excessively influence specific gatherings. Governmental policy regarding minorities in society approaches and variety drives are among the methodologies utilized to balance oppressive practices and advance equivalent open doors. Nonetheless, accomplishing work environment value requires progressing endeavors to address predispositions in enrollment, lay out straightforward compensation structures, and make comprehensive corporate societies.

Financial status is an unavoidable element impacting foundational disparities across different spaces. People from low-pay foundations face hindrances to getting to quality medical services, instructive open doors, and stable lodging. Breaking the pattern of neediness includes executing approaches that address financial inconsistencies, like raising the lowest pay permitted by law, guaranteeing reasonable lodging, and extending admittance to social administrations. An all encompassing way to deal with financial imbalance considers the interconnectedness of monetary, instructive, and wellbeing results.

Medical services incongruities are one more appearance of foundational imbalances. Minimized people group frequently experience higher paces of ongoing sicknesses, diminished admittance to medical care administrations, and abberations in wellbeing results. Tending to medical services disparities requires a complex methodology, including extending admittance to reasonable medical services, tending to social determinants of wellbeing, and advancing variety in the medical services labor force to guarantee socially equipped consideration.

Law enforcement frameworks universally wrestle with issues of fundamental separation, especially concerning racial and financial variations. Networks of variety frequently face higher paces of policing, more brutal condemning, and expanded imprisonment. Changing the law enforcement framework includes tending to foundational predispositions, putting resources into local area based options in contrast to imprisonment, and cultivating trust between policing minimized networks.

The multifacetedness of personalities intensifies foundational disparities, making special difficulties for people with different underestimated characters. For instance, a person who distinguishes as both a lady and an ethnic minority might confront particular types of segregation that emerge from the crossing point of orientation and race. Perceiving and tending to the convergences of character are fundamental for creating arrangements and drives that genuinely address the different requirements, everything being equal.

The job of institutional practices in sustaining foundational disparities couldn't possibly be more significant. Arrangements and methodology inside establishments, whether legislative, instructive, or corporate, may accidentally add to biased results. Resolving fundamental issues includes directing exhaustive evaluations of institutional works on, recognizing areas of inclination, and carrying out changes to guarantee reasonableness and inclusivity.

Regulation assumes a vital part in tending to fundamental disparities and segregation. Hostile to segregation regulations, governmental policy regarding minorities in society arrangements, and equivalent open door guidelines are among the legitimate apparatuses pointed toward amending authentic and primary treacheries. In any case, the adequacy of these regulations relies upon their implementation and flexibility to developing cultural standards. Ceaseless endeavors to reinforce and grow lawful systems are important to stay up with the changing scene of segregation.

Public mindfulness and promotion are essential parts of tending to fundamental imbalances. Grassroots developments, drove by impacted networks, frequently drive social change and push for strategy changes. Backing endeavors mean to enhance underestimated voices, bring issues to light about foundational issues, and activate public help for impartial approaches. Virtual entertainment stages, specifically, have become amazing assets for enhancing voices, sharing stories, and sorting out crusades that challenge fundamental imbalances.

Media portrayal assumes a huge part in molding public discernments and supporting or testing generalizations. Media that propagates destructive stories or neglects to precisely address different encounters can add to fundamental disparities. Advancing media proficiency, supporting different narrating, and considering news sources responsible for fair-minded detailing add to a more precise and comprehensive depiction of people and networks.

With regards to innovation, there is a developing acknowledgment of the potential for calculations and man-made consciousness to sustain foundational predispositions. From employing calculations that incidentally favor specific socioeconomics to facial acknowledgment programming that excessively misidentifies people from explicit racial foundations, the utilization of innovation can intensify existing imbalances. Guaranteeing moral and fair mechanical practices includes examining calculations for predisposition, advancing variety in the tech business, and creating vigorous guidelines.

Schooling and mindfulness inside the general set of laws are vital for tending to foundational imbalances. Judges, legal advisors, and policing should go through preparing to perceive and challenge their own predispositions. Carrying out supportive equity practices and local area policing models that focus on joint effort over corrective measures can assist with reshaping the law enforcement scene and encourage trust among networks and policing.

Repayments address a combative however significant part of tending to verifiable and progressing foundational imbalances. The idea of compensations includes recognizing verifiable treacheries, like bondage and colonization, and carrying out measures to correct their persevering through influences. Repayments might take different structures, including monetary pay, instructive open doors, and designated interests in minimized networks. The discussion around restitutions highlights the intricacies of reviewing verifiable and foundational treacheries.

Worldwide participation is fundamental in tending to foundational imbalances, as many issues rise above public boundaries. Worldwide associations, settlements, and discretionary endeavors are essential for organizing reactions to worldwide difficulties, for example, destitution, environmental change, and denials of basic freedoms. Perceiving the interconnectedness of fundamental issues considers cooperative endeavors that influence assorted points of view and assets.

Disparities and separation comprise tenacious difficulties that saturate different parts of society, molding the encounters and chances of people in light of elements like race, orientation, financial status, and that's just the beginning. These issues are well established in verifiable traditions of fundamental persecution and keep on appearing across different spaces, including training, business, medical services, law enforcement, and then some. Understanding the nuanced manners by which imbalances and separation work is essential for creating powerful procedures that advance value, equity, and inclusivity.

Verifiable setting plays a primary job in figuring out contemporary disparities. Hundreds of years of expansionism, subjection, and regulated separation have left enduring engravings on friendly designs, adding to settled in differences that continue today. Perceiving the verifiable foundations of disparities is fundamental for destroying the fundamental boundaries that ruin specific gatherings from getting to valuable open doors and assets.

Race stays a focal hub around which numerous imbalances rotate. Networks of variety frequently face unbalanced difficulties, going from lower admittance to quality training and medical care to expanded paces of policing and detainment. Segregation in light of race limits individual open doors as well as propagates foundational differences that influence whole networks. Tending to racial disparities requires a complete methodology that challenges prejudicial practices, advances equivalent portrayal, and addresses the underlying drivers of foundational bigotry.

Orientation inconsistencies address one more component of disparities and segregation. Ladies, internationally, face a large number of difficulties, including wage holes, restricted admittance to administrative roles, and orientation based savagery. Diversity assumes a basic part in figuring out the exceptional encounters of ladies from various racial, ethnic, and financial foundations. Support for orientation balance includes testing cultural standards, advancing comprehensive arrangements, and establishing conditions where ladies can flourish by and by and expertly.

Financial status is an unavoidable element that impacts valuable open doors and results across different spaces. People from low-pay foundations frequently experience hindrances to quality training, medical services, and stable lodging. Monetary imbalance adds to a pattern of drawback, restricting the vertical portability of underestimated networks. Tending to financial imbalances includes executing approaches that tackle the main drivers of destitution, give social wellbeing nets, and make pathways to monetary strengthening.

In the domain of training, disparities and separation manifest in different structures. Schools in financially distraught regions might need assets, experienced educators, and extracurricular open doors, adding to variations in instructive results. Separation inside instructive organizations can likewise appear as one-sided disciplinary practices and restricted admittance to cutting edge courses. Making an impartial schooling system includes tending to asset incongruities, executing comprehensive educational plans, and cultivating conditions that focus on variety and inclusivity.

Work rehearses assume a huge part in sustaining or testing imbalances. Separation in recruiting, wage holes, and restricted open doors for professional success lopsidedly influence specific gatherings. Governmental policy regarding minorities in society strategies and variety drives expect to check prejudicial practices and advance equivalent open doors in the working environment. Nonetheless, destroying foundational separation requires progressing endeavors to address predispositions in enrollment, lay out straightforward compensation structures, and make comprehensive corporate societies.

Medical services differences are one more basic part of disparities and segregation. Underestimated people group frequently face higher paces of ongoing sicknesses, decreased admittance to medical care administrations, and less fortunate wellbeing results.

Social determinants of wellbeing, like admittance to training, work, and lodging, add to these variations. Addressing medical services disparities includes extending admittance to reasonable medical services, tending to social determinants of wellbeing, and advancing variety in the medical care labor force to guarantee socially equipped consideration.

Law enforcement frameworks around the world wrestle with issues of fundamental separation, especially concerning racial and financial differences. Networks of variety frequently face higher paces of policing, more brutal condemning, and expanded imprisonment. Improving the law enforcement framework includes tending to foundational predispositions, putting resources into local area based options in contrast to detainment, and cultivating trust between policing minimized networks.

The multifacetedness of characters intensifies the intricacies of disparities and separation. People with different minimized personalities might confront remarkable difficulties that emerge from the convergence of race, orientation, financial status, sexual direction, and the sky is the limit from there. Perceiving and tending to these convergences is fundamental for creating approaches and drives that genuinely address the different requirements, everything being equal.

In the domain of innovation, there is a developing acknowledgment of the potential for calculations and man-made consciousness to sustain foundational predispositions. From employing calculations that unintentionally favor specific socioeconomics to facial acknowledgment programming that excessively misidentifies people from explicit racial foundations, the utilization of innovation can intensify existing imbalances. Guaranteeing moral and fair mechanical practices includes examining calculations for predisposition, advancing variety in the tech business, and creating vigorous guidelines.

Public mindfulness and backing assume vital parts in tending to disparities and segregation. Grassroots developments, drove by impacted networks, frequently drive social change and push for strategy changes. Promotion endeavors mean to intensify underestimated voices, bring issues to light about fundamental issues, and activate public help for fair arrangements. Web-based entertainment stages have become useful assets for intensifying voices, sharing stories, and coordinating efforts that challenge disparities.

Media portrayal assumes a huge part in molding public discernments and building up or testing generalizations. Media that sustains unsafe accounts or neglects to precisely address assorted encounters can add to foundational imbalances. Advancing media proficiency, supporting different narrating, and considering news sources responsible for fair detailing add to a more exact and comprehensive depiction of people and networks.

Legitimate structures and regulation are critical devices for tending to fundamental disparities and segregation. Hostile to separation regulations, governmental policy regarding minorities in society strategies, and equivalent open door guidelines are among the lawful apparatuses pointed toward correcting verifiable and underlying treacheries. Nonetheless, the adequacy of these regulations relies upon their requirement and versatility to developing cultural standards. Nonstop endeavors to reinforce and extend lawful systems are important to stay up with the changing scene of segregation.

Repayments address a petulant yet significant part of tending to verifiable and continuous foundational disparities. The idea of compensations includes recognizing verifiable shameful acts, like servitude and colonization, and executing measures to redress their persevering through influences. Repayments might take different structures, including monetary remuneration, instructive open doors, and designated interests in underestimated networks. The discussion around restitutions highlights the intricacies of reviewing verifiable and fundamental treacheries.

Worldwide collaboration is fundamental in tending to foundational imbalances, as many issues rise above public lines. Worldwide associations, deals, and strategic endeavors are pivotal for organizing reactions to worldwide difficulties, for example, destitution, environmental change, and denials of basic liberties. Perceiving the interconnectedness of foundational issues considers cooperative endeavors that influence different viewpoints and assets.

Chapter 7

Global Perspectives on Human Rights

Common liberties, an idea well established in the standards of uniformity, respect, and equity, have developed over hundreds of years, rising above social and geological limits. As the world turns out to be progressively interconnected, the significance of a worldwide viewpoint on basic freedoms couldn't possibly be more significant. This exposition plans to investigate different elements of common freedoms from a worldwide point of view, diving into verifiable settings, contemporary difficulties, and the job of global establishments in advancing and safeguarding these essential privileges.

The underlying foundations of the advanced common freedoms system can be followed back to the result of The Second Great War. The monstrosities committed during the conflict provoked the global local area to perceive the requirement for an exhaustive framework that would shield the inborn poise and worth of each and every person. The Widespread Statement of Common freedoms (UDHR), embraced by the Unified Countries General Gathering in 1948, remains as a fantastic achievement in the mission for worldwide basic liberties norms.

The UDHR, a non-restricting statement, laid the foundation for ensuing global common liberties instruments and deals. Its introduction persuasively explains the common vision of a reality where individuals appreciate opportunity, equity, and harmony. While the UDHR was a critical step in the right direction, the way to worldwide basic liberties security has been full of difficulties, mirroring the complicated exchange of social, political, and financial elements.

One of the getting through difficulties in the worldwide talk on common freedoms is the pressure among universalism and social relativism. The possibility of all inclusive basic freedoms attests that specific privileges are intrinsic to all people by excellence of their mankind, regardless of social or provincial contrasts. Then again, social relativism fights that basic freedoms ought to be perceived inside the setting of explicit social, authentic, and social foundations.

Exploring this pressure is a fragile errand, as it requires finding some kind of harmony between regarding social variety and maintaining a typical norm of basic freedoms. Pundits contend that the burden of Western-driven values might prompt social colonialism, sabotaging the authenticity of the basic liberties structure in assorted social orders. Alternately, defenders of universalism contend that specific privileges, like the right to life and independence from torment, ought to be non-debatable and material all around.

The battle to accommodate these viewpoints is obvious in discusses encompassing issues like opportunity of articulation, orientation fairness, and LGBTQ+ freedoms. While the UDHR champions the right to opportunity of assessment and articulation, social standards and political systems frequently conflict with this guideline. Control, concealment of contradiction, and limitations on the media persevere in different areas of the planet, testing the comprehensiveness of these privileges.

Likewise, the quest for orientation uniformity as a basic freedom experiences social obstruction and firmly established man centric designs. Practices like female genital mutilation, kid marriage, and orientation based viciousness persevere, featuring the requirement for a nuanced comprehension of social settings without compromising the center standards of common freedoms.

The LGBTQ+ freedoms development further highlights the conflict between social relativism and universalism. In numerous social orders, homosexuality is derided or condemned in view of social or strict convictions. Advocates for LGBTQ+ freedoms contend that the option to cherish and communicate one's personality rises above social contrasts, accentuating the general idea of specific common liberties.

The worldwide viewpoint on common freedoms likewise wrestles with monetary differences and their effect on the happiness regarding privileges. Monetary, social, and social freedoms, as expressed in the Worldwide Contract on Financial, Social and Social Privileges (ICESCR), feature the right to training, work, and a satisfactory way of life.

Nonetheless, millions all over the planet actually face outrageous neediness, absence of admittance to schooling, and lacking medical services, representing the diligent hole between common liberties goals and reality.

The multifacetedness of basic freedoms becomes evident while thinking about what issues like neediness excessively mean for minimized gatherings. Native populaces, ethnic minorities, and exiles frequently face foundational segregation, restricting their admittance to essential privileges. The worldwide local area's obligation to basic freedoms requires tending to the side effects as well as the underlying drivers of disparity and bad form.

Worldwide organizations assume a urgent part in forming and upholding worldwide common freedoms principles. The Unified Countries, with its different particular offices and bodies, fills in as a focal center point for organizing endeavors to advance and safeguard basic freedoms. The UN Basic liberties Committee, laid out in 2006, assumes a key part in tending to common freedoms infringement, leading occasional surveys of part states, and cultivating exchange on squeezing common freedoms issues.

Provincial associations additionally add to the worldwide basic liberties scene. The European Court of Common liberties, the Between American Court of Basic freedoms, and the African Commission on Human and People groups' Privileges are instances of local bodies that arbitrate basic liberties cases inside their separate purviews. These foundations supplement the more extensive system laid out by the UDHR and add to the advancement of provincial basic freedoms standards.

Notwithstanding the endeavors of global and local foundations, the adequacy of basic liberties instruments faces huge difficulties. The rule of state power frequently conflicts with the command of these bodies, as states might oppose outside examination of their homegrown undertakings. Additionally, the authorization systems of global basic freedoms regulation are frequently condemned for their restricted capacity to consider culprits responsible.

The idea of philanthropic mediation brings up complex moral and legitimate issues with regards to basic freedoms. While the global local area has an honest conviction to forestall and answer mass barbarities, the utilization of power to safeguard common liberties is laden with chances. The mediations in Kosovo, Libya, and Iraq have created banters about the authenticity and unseen side-effects of military activities embraced for the sake of basic freedoms.

The ascent of populism and patriotism in different areas of the planet represents one more test to the worldwide basic freedoms plan. Pioneers who focus on public interests over worldwide collaboration might subvert the viability of foundations committed to maintaining basic freedoms. The disintegration of multilateralism and the withdrawal of specific countries from peaceful accords signal an unsettling pattern that could subvert the aggregate endeavors to address worldwide difficulties.

In the computerized age, innovation acquaints new aspects with the talk on basic freedoms. The right to protection, opportunity of demeanor, and admittance to data face uncommon difficulties in the time of observation, information mining, and online oversight. Issues like the spread of disinformation, cyberattacks, and the utilization of man-made consciousness in reconnaissance raise moral worries that request worldwide consideration and cooperative arrangements.

The worldwide viewpoint on basic liberties additionally envelops the situation of outcasts and travelers. Constrained dislodging, whether because of contention, oppression, or ecological elements, represents a helpful emergency that tests the global local area's obligation to safeguarding the privileges of weak populaces. The Outcast Show and its convention give a lawful structure to the security of exiles, however the size of contemporary removal requires inventive and helpful ways to deal with address the underlying drivers and give sturdy arrangements.

Natural corruption and environmental change arise as interconnected issues with significant ramifications for basic freedoms. The right to a sound climate, as a basic piece of the right to life and prosperity, is progressively perceived in worldwide regulation. Environment actuated relocation, asset shortage, and the lopsided effect of ecological corruption on underestimated networks highlight the earnestness of coordinating natural contemplations into the common freedoms system.

The job of companies in the worldwide basic freedoms scene has acquired conspicuousness lately. Transnational enterprises work across borders, frequently in locales with feeble administration and remiss administrative systems. The effect of corporate exercises on basic freedoms, whether through ecological contamination, work double-dealing, or complicity in denials of basic freedoms, requires a nearer assessment of the obligations and responsibility of companies in maintaining common liberties norms.

Common society assumes a fundamental part in propelling the worldwide basic freedoms plan. Non-legislative associations (NGOs), grassroots developments, and common liberties safeguards add to checking, support, and responsibility. The space for common society, notwithstanding, is contracting in many areas of the planet, with expanding limitations on opportunity of affiliation, articulation, and serene gathering. The worldwide local area's obligation to common liberties should incorporate powerful help for common society entertainers who frequently work at the very front of freedoms insurance.

7.1 Comparative analysis of human rights practices in different regions

The security and advancement of basic freedoms address a complicated and diverse test for countries across the globe. Varieties in social, verifiable, and political settings add to unique common freedoms rehearses in various locales. A near examination of these practices reveals insight into both the headway made and the persevering difficulties looked chasing a widespread norm for basic liberties.

Starting with Western nations, especially those in Europe, a verifiable tradition of Illumination goals and popularity based administration has formed their way to deal with common freedoms. The European Association (EU) plays had a focal impact in cultivating a typical common liberties system among its part states. The European Show on Basic freedoms (ECHR), regulated by the European Court of Common liberties (ECtHR), lays out a lawful structure that considers part states responsible for common liberties infringement.

Scandinavian nations, frequently refered to as models in basic freedoms rehearses, focus on friendly and monetary privileges close by common and political privileges. Sweden, Norway, Denmark, and Finland reliably rank high on worldwide common liberties files, flaunting powerful friendly government assistance frameworks, orientation uniformity, and comprehensive strategies. Notwithstanding, challenges persevere, for example, issues connected with the treatment of refuge searchers and rising xenophobia.

In Southern Europe, nations like Italy, Spain, and Greece have confronted difficulties in overseeing movement streams and tending to monetary variations. The Mediterranean locale fills in as a point of convergence for the crossing point of basic freedoms, movement, and boundary control. Worries about the treatment of transients, including cases of pushbacks and deficient everyday environments, highlight the intricacies of offsetting public interests with common freedoms commitments.

Moving to Eastern Europe, the traditions of dictator rule and Soviet impact have left enduring engravings on common liberties rehearses. Post-socialist changes have been set apart by endeavors to line up with European common liberties guidelines, however issues like media opportunity, legal freedom, and minority privileges keep on presenting difficulties. Nations like Hungary and Poland have confronted analysis for measures apparent as subverting majority rule establishments and common freedoms insurances.

In North America, the US and Canada present fascinating relative elements. The U.S., while maintaining areas of strength for an of common freedoms, has confronted examination for issues like racial disparity, mass detainment, and the utilization of capital punishment. The intricacies of offsetting public safety worries with individual privileges have been obvious in discusses encompassing reconnaissance rehearses and the treatment of prisoners.

Canada, then again, frequently underscores a multicultural and comprehensive way to deal with common liberties. Its Contract of Privileges and Opportunities ensures central privileges and opportunities, and the nation has been proactive in tending to authentic treacheries, including the treatment of Native people groups. Notwithstanding, challenges persevere in regions like the privileges of Native people group, especially with respect to land freedoms and self-assurance.

In Latin America, the tradition of tyrant systems and extended clashes has altogether impacted basic freedoms elements. Momentary equity processes have been urgent in tending to authentic monstrosities, with nations like Argentina and Chile gaining ground in considering culprits responsible. Be that as it may, challenges endure, including issues connected with police viciousness, defilement, and the security of basic liberties protectors.

Venezuela has gathered worldwide consideration for its common liberties circumstance, set apart by political constraint, financial emergencies, and a philanthropic crisis. The complex political scene has prompted captivated accounts, with some contending that outside entertainers compound the circumstance, while others underline the requirement for worldwide intercession to safeguard common liberties.

In Africa, the common freedoms scene is assorted, mirroring the landmass' rich embroidery of societies, accounts, and administration models. South Africa's change from politically-sanctioned racial segregation to a majority rule government represents a pledge to common liberties and compromise. In any case, challenges persevere across the mainland, including clashes, dictator rule, and issues connected with opportunity of articulation and get together.

The African Sanction on Human and People groups' Freedoms, embraced by the African Association (AU), gives a local system to basic liberties. However, execution shifts, and concerns emerge in regards to the autonomy of legal authorities, media opportunity, and the assurance of weak gatherings. The circumstance in nations like Sudan, Ethiopia, and Nigeria features the intricacies of adjusting security and common freedoms in assorted settings.

The Center East presents a perplexing scene set apart by international pressures, dictator administration, and clashes. The Bedouin Spring uprisings of 2011 reflected yearnings for popularity based changes and common freedoms enhancements. Be that as it may, the results have been changed, for certain nations encountering political advances, while others saw expanded constraint and savagery.

Israel and the involved Palestinian regions stand at the convergence of basic liberties and extended struggle. The Israeli-Palestinian struggle brings up complex issues about self-assurance, security, and the freedoms of the two Israelis and Palestinians. Global associations, including the Unified Countries, routinely survey basic liberties conditions in the district, yet accomplishing an extensive and enduring goal stays subtle.

Asia, with its different exhibit of societies and administration models, presents a changed basic freedoms scene. East Asian nations like Japan and South Korea have taken monetary steps close by endeavors to address verifiable treacheries. Nonetheless, concerns continue, especially in regards to issues like separation, treatment of minority gatherings, and verifiable memory.

China's basic liberties rehearses stand out, with discusses zeroing in on issues like political suppression, strict opportunity, and the treatment of ethnic minorities, eminently the Uighurs. The Chinese government affirms that its methodology is established in social and verifiable settings, underscoring strength and improvement.

In Southeast Asia, nations like Singapore, Malaysia, and Thailand explore common liberties challenges inside different political frameworks. Dictator propensities, limitations on opportunity of articulation, and issues connected with transient work highlight the intricacies of advancing and safeguarding basic freedoms in the district.

In South Asia, India, the world's biggest majority rules government, wrestles with a scope of common liberties issues. The country's lively common society, autonomous legal executive, and free media coincide with difficulties connected with position based separation, strict pressures, and issues influencing minimized networks. The circumstance in Kashmir and worries about opportunity of articulation have been subjects of worldwide examination.

All in all, a similar examination of common freedoms rehearses in various locales uncovers a mind boggling exchange of verifiable, social, and political elements. While specific all inclusive standards support basic liberties, their understanding and execution differ generally. Western nations, with their vote based customs, have taken huge steps yet face difficulties in regions like movement and racial imbalance. Momentary equity processes in Latin America exhibit the significance of tending to authentic shameful acts, while Africa explores assorted difficulties, from clashes to administration issues.

The Center East wrestles with the intricacies of political changes and extended clashes, while Asia presents a range of administration models, from vote based to dictator. Every area faces special difficulties, requiring custom fitted methodologies that regard social variety while maintaining all inclusive basic liberties standards. The worldwide local area's obligation to basic freedoms requires progressing exchange, co-operation, and a common perspective of the developing elements molding the quest for an all the more and evenhanded world for all.

7.2 Highlighting success stories and areas that require improvement

Looking at the worldwide scene of basic liberties uncovers a nuanced story that incorporates both examples of overcoming adversity and industrious difficulties. While steps have been made in different locales, certain regions require constant consideration and improvement to guarantee the acknowledgment of widespread common liberties norms. This examination will highlight examples of overcoming adversity and recognize key regions where purposeful endeavors are fundamental.

Examples of overcoming adversity:

1. **Momentary Equity in Latin America:**
   Latin American nations, including Argentina and Chile, have gained critical headway in tending to authentic shameful acts through momentary equity processes. Truth and compromise commissions, alongside preliminaries of culprits, have added to recognizing past outrages and encouraging a culture of responsibility. These endeavors act as models for different districts wrestling with the consequence of struggles or harsh systems.

2. **Orientation Fairness in the Nordic Nations:**
   Nordic nations, like Sweden, Norway, Denmark, and Finland, have reliably shown a pledge to orientation correspondence. Hearty social arrangements, comprehensive administration, and proactive measures to address working environment orientation differences have prompted elevated degrees of orientation equity in these countries. Ladies' support in political, financial, and social circles is significant, setting benchmarks for orientation comprehensive practices worldwide.

3. **Popularity based Changes in South Africa:**
   South Africa's progress from politically-sanctioned racial segregation to a vote based system remains as a demonstration of the extraordinary force of compromise and comprehensive administration. Reality and Compromise Commission, drove by Ecclesiastical overseer Desmond Tutu, assumed a critical part in tending to verifiable treacheries. The foundation of a vote based government and the consideration of recently minimized networks in the political cycle embody effective country building endeavors.

4. **European Association and Common freedoms System:**
   The European Association (EU) has been instrumental in making a typical

common freedoms system among its part states. The European Show on Common freedoms (ECHR) and the European Court of Basic liberties (ECtHR) give a legitimate establishment to safeguarding common freedoms. The EU's accentuation on law and order, vote based administration, and collaboration has added to the headway of common liberties inside its part states.

5. **Admittance to Schooling in A few Asian Nations:**

Certain Asian nations have gained honorable headway in extending admittance to training. Countries like South Korea and Japan have put essentially in schooling systems, prompting high proficiency rates and instructive results. Endeavors to guarantee equivalent admittance to training for all, paying little mind to orientation or financial foundation, act as sure models in the more extensive setting of common liberties.

Regions Requiring Improvement:

1. **Traveler and Exile Freedoms Worldwide:**
   Perhaps of the most squeezing challenge on the worldwide common freedoms plan is the treatment of transients and outcasts. Across different districts, there are occasions of insufficient day to day environments, absence of admittance to fundamental administrations, and common freedoms infringement against travelers and exiles. The requirement for far reaching and merciful ways to deal with movement, grounded in regard for human nobility, stays a basic region requiring improvement.

2. **Opportunity of Articulation in the Advanced Age:**
   The coming of the computerized age has carried new difficulties to the security of opportunity of articulation. Occasions of online control, observation, and the concealment of difference present dangers to people's privileges to unreservedly offer their viewpoints. Adjusting the requirement for network safety with the security of principal freedoms requires imaginative arrangements and a reexamination of legitimate systems to guarantee that common liberties are maintained in the computerized circle.

3. **Native Freedoms and Land Questions:**
   Native people group overall keep on confronting difficulties connected with land freedoms, social protection, and acknowledgment of their independence. From the Americas to Asia and Africa, land questions frequently bring about the removal of native people groups, compromising their conventional lifestyles. Reinforcing lawful structures and guaranteeing significant support of native networks in dynamic cycles are fundamental stages toward resolving these relentless issues.

4. **Segregation and Viciousness Against Minorities:**
   Segregation and viciousness against minority bunches endure in different districts, influencing ethnic, strict, and sexual minorities. From against LGBTQ+

separation to strict mistreatment, minimized networks frequently endure the worst part of fundamental predispositions. Reinforcing lawful assurances, cultivating comprehensive instruction, and battling cultural biases are critical stages toward making social orders where all people appreciate equivalent freedoms and security.

5. **Dictatorship and Disintegration of Common Freedoms:**
The ascent of dictator propensities in certain districts represents a critical danger to basic freedoms. Disintegration of common freedoms, limitations on opportunity of articulation, and the debilitating of popularity based organizations are patterns seen in a few nations. Addressing these difficulties requires a deliberate work to maintain vote based values, reinforce balanced governance, and engage common society to oppose the infringement of dictatorship.

6. **Natural and Environment Equity:**
The crossing point of ecological debasement and basic liberties, especially with regards to environmental change, requests expanded consideration. Weak people group, frequently the most un-answerable for ecological debasement, endure the worst part of environment actuated debacles and asset exhaustion. Integrating natural equity standards into basic liberties structures is fundamental for tending to the interconnected difficulties of ecological supportability and common freedoms.

7. **Financial Differences and Social Privileges:**
While progress has been made in perceiving common and political privileges, financial, social, and social freedoms stay slippery for some.
Resolving issues like neediness, inconsistent admittance to medical services and training, and work double-dealing requires a comprehensive way to deal with common liberties. Shutting the hole between common liberties beliefs and the financial truth of weak populaces is quite difficult for the worldwide local area.

8. **Insurance of Common liberties Safeguards:**

Basic liberties safeguards, including activists, writers, and common society pioneers, face expanding dangers and goes after all around the world. The contracting space for common society in certain districts, combined with the focusing of people upholding for basic liberties, represents a critical test. Reinforcing components for the security of common liberties protectors and guaranteeing their capacity to work unafraid of backlashes are urgent parts of encouraging a dynamic common society.

In exploring the complicated territory of worldwide common freedoms, recognizing examples of overcoming adversity is essentially as significant as tending to regions that require improvement. From fruitful momentary equity processes in Latin America to steps in orientation balance in the Nordic nations, positive models enlighten the way ahead. Be that as it may, the relentless difficulties, including the treatment of transients, disintegration of common freedoms, and oppression minorities, highlight the continuous requirement for cautiousness and deliberate endeavors.

The worldwide local area should participate in cooperative exchange, share best practices, and consider each other responsible to maintain the standards cherished in global basic freedoms instruments. Gaining from triumphs and addressing inadequacies on the whole will add to building an existence where the inborn pride and privileges of each and every individual are perceived as well as completely understood. Chasing an all the more and fair worldwide society, the double spotlight on victories and regions requiring improvement stays central.

7.3 The role of diplomacy and international cooperation

Discretion and worldwide collaboration are foundations of the worldwide request, assuming urgent parts in forming relations among countries and tending to complex difficulties that rise above borders. This article investigates the complex components of discretion and worldwide collaboration, looking at their verifiable development, contemporary importance, and the job they play in resolving squeezing worldwide issues.

Authentic Development of Discretion:

Tact, as an instrument of statecraft, has a rich verifiable heredity tracing all the way back to old civic establishments. The act of sending emissaries to arrange deals and partnerships is obvious in the authentic records of Mesopotamia, Egypt, and China. As social orders developed, so did discretionary practices, with the rise of formalized conciliatory missions, consulates, and arrangements during the Renaissance in Europe.

The Tranquility of Westphalia in 1648 is much of the time thought about a turning point in the improvement of current strategy. This series of arrangements denoted the finish of the Thirty Years' Conflict and laid out the standards of state sway and nonmediation in homegrown undertakings, laying the foundation for the Westphalian framework. Resulting hundreds of years saw the codification of discretionary standards, the foundation of the Vienna Congress in 1815, and the development of current tact as a calling.

Contemporary Meaning of Strategy:

In the contemporary worldwide scene, strategy stays a key part in global relations. States utilize strategy to propel their public advantages, fabricate coalitions, and explore complex international difficulties. Representatives act as conductors of correspondence between countries, arranging arrangements, settling debates, and cultivating understanding. The job of tact reaches out past conventional statecraft to incorporate a wide exhibit of entertainers, like worldwide associations, non-legislative associations (NGOs), and global enterprises.

Multilateral discretion, worked with through organizations like the Assembled Countries (UN), has become progressively significant in resolving worldwide issues. The UN fills in as a gathering for discretionary commitment, giving a stage to exchange, compromise, and cooperative endeavors to handle shared difficulties. Particular offices inside the UN, like the World Wellbeing Association (WHO) and the Global Nuclear Energy Organization (IAEA), embody the different jobs of tact in regions going from general wellbeing to atomic restraint.

The Job of Worldwide Collaboration:

Worldwide collaboration, firmly interweaved with strategy, is a critical component for tending to worldwide difficulties that rise above public boundaries. It includes coordinated endeavors by different entertainers, including states, global associations, and non-state substances, to accomplish shared objectives. The significance of global participation has become dramatically as the world has become more interconnected, with issues like environmental change, pandemics, and psychological warfare requiring cooperative arrangements.

1. **Environmental Change and Ecological Collaboration:**

   Environmental change represents the requirement for hearty worldwide participation. The Paris Understanding, took on in 2015, addresses a milestone discretionary accomplishment in the battle against environmental change. The agreement, endorsed by almost 200 nations, plans to restrict worldwide temperature increments and alleviate the effects of environmental change. Worldwide collaboration in this setting includes sharing logical information, innovation move, and monetary help to assist emerging countries with progressing to supportable practices.

   Regardless of strategic triumphs, for example, the Paris Arrangement, challenges continue accomplishing worldwide agreement on aggressive environment activity. Differences in commitments, especially among created and agricultural countries, highlight the intricacy of adjusting different interests.

   Worldwide participation in the domain of environmental change requires continuous political endeavors to connect these holes and execute successful measures to defend the planet.

2. **General Wellbeing and Worldwide Pandemics:**

   The episode of worldwide pandemics, for example, the Coronavirus emergency, highlights the basic job of global participation and strategy in tending to wellbeing crises. The World Wellbeing Association (WHO) fills in as a focal center for worldwide wellbeing discretion, organizing reactions, sharing data, and working with joint effort among countries. Political endeavors are significant in guaranteeing the fair dispersion of antibodies, assembling assets, and exploring the intricacies of general wellbeing emergencies.

   The Coronavirus pandemic likewise uncovered weaknesses in the worldwide wellbeing administration framework and featured the requirement for changes. Conciliatory drives pointed toward reinforcing global participation in wellbeing administration, working on early advance notice frameworks, and supporting the versatility of medical services foundation are fundamental for forestalling and alleviating future pandemics.

3. **Atomic Restraint and Arms Control:**
Discretion plays had a focal impact in endeavors to forestall the multiplication of atomic weapons and advance arms control. Settlements like the Deal on the Restraint of Atomic Weapons (NPT) epitomize political undertakings to check the spread of atomic capacities. Worldwide collaboration in this space includes demilitarization discussions, check components, and conciliatory exchanges to address territorial pressures that could grow into atomic struggles.

Notwithstanding, the demilitarization plan faces difficulties, with atomic furnished states modernizing their weapons stores and the development of new international elements. Conciliatory drives, for example, the Exhaustive Atomic Test-Boycott Deal (CTBT) and the Settlement on the Restriction of Atomic Weapons (TPNW), reflect continuous endeavors to reinforce the standardizing system against atomic weapons and advance the objective of a world liberated from the danger of atomic fighting.

4. **Basic liberties and Discretion:**
Strategy assumes a significant part in advancing and safeguarding basic liberties on the worldwide stage. Reciprocal and multilateral political commitment give gatherings to tending to basic liberties infringement, pushing for equity, and considering culprits responsible. Global associations like the UN Common liberties Gathering conduct occasional surveys of part states' basic freedoms records, encouraging strategic discoursed on common liberties issues.

Notwithstanding, the crossing point of tact and common liberties can be mind boggling. States might focus on public interests over basic liberties contemplations, prompting occasions where strategic sober mindedness beats moral goals. Finding some kind of harmony between conciliatory commitment and maintaining common freedoms standards requires nuanced approaches and supported endeavors to coordinate basic liberties contemplations into political techniques.

5. **Monetary Participation and Exchange Strategy:**

Monetary strategy and worldwide exchange are necessary parts of political commitment, forming worldwide financial relations and encouraging participation. Economic alliance, haggled through conciliatory channels, expect to advance monetary development, work with the development of labor and products, and make a system for settling debates. Foundations like the World Exchange Association (WTO) act as stages for conciliatory discussions and the goal of exchange related issues.

Monetary collaboration likewise stretches out to advancement help, where more prosperous countries offer help to agricultural nations. Conciliatory endeavors in this domain include arranging help bundles, obligation alleviation, and supportable improvement drives. Nonetheless, monetary collaboration faces difficulties connected with exchange awkward nature, protectionism, and the lopsided dissemination of financial advantages, requiring continuous conciliatory endeavors to resolve these issues.

Difficulties to Discretion and Worldwide Participation:

While strategy and worldwide participation are vital devices for tending to worldwide difficulties, they face a few difficulties that ruin their viability.

1. **Patriotism and Disintegration of Multilateralism:**

   The ascent of patriotism in certain nations has prompted a retreat from multilateralism, testing the viability of global collaboration. The prioritization of public interests over aggregate activity can subvert strategic endeavors to address shared difficulties. Cases of nations pulling out from peaceful accords or establishments signal a shift away from cooperative methodologies, presenting difficulties to the soul of collaboration.

2. **International Strains and Power Elements:**

   International strains and power elements among significant states can obstruct viable discretion. Contending interests, verifiable complaints, and vital competitions make deterrents to political goals of contentions and worldwide difficulties. Negotiators frequently wrestle with exploring complex international scenes where public interests might overshadow helpful undertakings.

3. **Absence of Authorization Systems:**

   While peaceful accords and deals are fundamental conciliatory devices, their viability relies upon the presence of powerful requirement systems. At times, the shortfall of solid authorization systems restricts the capacity to consider states responsible for infringement. Discretionary endeavors to resolve issues like denials of basic freedoms or ecological debasement might experience difficulties when states see negligible ramifications for resistance.

4. **Imbalance and Worldwide Variations:**

   Worldwide imbalances in monetary turn of events, admittance to assets, and mechanical abilities present difficulties to global participation. Agricultural nations might confront troubles in completely taking part in strategic exchanges or carrying out worldwide drives because of asset requirements and primary abberations. Spanning these holes requires strategic endeavors to address underlying drivers and advance comprehensive collaboration.

5. **Network protection Dangers and Data Fighting:**

   The computerized age has acquainted new difficulties with strategy, especially in the domains of network protection and data fighting. Representatives should fight with the weaponization of data, cyberattacks, and the utilization of innovation to subvert political endeavors. Building standards and arrangements to administer the internet is a continuous strategic test, requiring aggregate activity to address arising dangers to worldwide security.

6. **Environment of Question and Conciliatory Breakdowns:**

In certain examples, an environment of question among countries can prompt conciliatory breakdowns. Arguments about domain, verifiable complaints, or political philosophies might obstruct compelling correspondence and joint effort. Reconstructing trust and cultivating open political channels become fundamental essentials for settling clashes and progressing shared objectives.

Strategy and global collaboration are basic apparatuses in exploring the intricacies of the interconnected world. From addressing environmental change and worldwide wellbeing emergencies to advancing basic liberties and forestalling furnished clashes, the progress of strategic undertakings depends on cooperation, discourse, and a guarantee to shared values.

While there have been eminent triumphs, relentless difficulties require discretionary resourcefulness and a recharged devotion to multilateralism. Beating patriotism, tending to drive irregular characteristics, and creating hearty requirement components are fundamental stages in improving the viability of strategic drives. The developing idea of worldwide difficulties requests versatile and imaginative conciliatory methodologies, supported by a mutual perspective that global collaboration isn't simply a decision yet a need for a safer, just, and economical world.

Worldwide participation remains as a foundation of worldwide administration, mirroring the interconnectedness of countries and the acknowledgment that tending to complex difficulties requires cooperative endeavors. This exposition dives into the multi-layered elements of worldwide collaboration, investigating its authentic roots, contemporary importance, and the difficulties and amazing open doors it presents on the worldwide stage.

Authentic Underpinnings of Global Participation:

The underlying foundations of worldwide participation can be followed back to old human advancements that took part in exchange, discretion, and social trades. Notwithstanding, the rise of formalized global participation picked up speed in the fallout of obliterating clashes, especially The Second Great War and The Second Great War. The Class of Countries, laid out after The Second Great War, was an early effort to encourage aggregate security and collaboration yet confronted constraints in forestalling the episode of another worldwide clash.

The Unified Countries (UN), laid out in 1945 following The Second Great War, addresses a urgent improvement in the development of worldwide participation. Cherished in the UN Contract are rules that highlight the significance of quiet goal of struggles, regard for common liberties, and worldwide collaboration to address worldwide difficulties. The UN fills in as a stage for discretionary exchange, struggle counteraction, and cooperative drives in regions like turn of events, wellbeing, and ecological maintainability.

Contemporary Meaning of Global Participation:

In the contemporary worldwide scene, global participation has become progressively imperative in tending to a variety of interconnected difficulties. The difficulties of the 21st 100 years, from environmental change to pandemics, rise above public lines, requiring aggregate activity and facilitated reactions. In this unique circumstance, worldwide associations, settlements, and strategic commitment assume crucial parts in molding a cooperative structure for worldwide administration.

1. **Environmental Change and Natural Participation:**

   Environmental change stands apart as perhaps of the most squeezing worldwide test that highlights the basic of global participation. The Paris Understanding, embraced in 2015, addresses a milestone political accomplishment in the domain of natural participation. Almost 200 nations vowed to restrict worldwide temperature increments and upgrade versatility to the effects of environmental change. The understanding represents the force of worldwide collaboration in making an aggregate reaction to an existential danger that rises above public limits.

   Compelling ecological participation reaches out past environmental change and incorporates endeavors to address biodiversity misfortune, deforestation, and contamination. Cooperative drives are urgent for the protection of shared assets and the advancement of supportable practices. Conciliatory endeavors in this space include arranging arrangements, setting global guidelines, and preparing monetary assets to help harmless to the ecosystem drives, all pointed toward accomplishing a harmony between human turn of events and biological supportability.

2. **General Wellbeing and Worldwide Wellbeing Collaboration:**

   Worldwide wellbeing collaboration has acquired unmistakable quality, especially with regards to the Coronavirus pandemic.

   The World Wellbeing Association (WHO), as a particular organization of the UN, assumes a focal part in planning global reactions to wellbeing emergencies. The pandemic featured the interconnectedness of general wellbeing and the need of cross-line collaboration in forestalling, alleviating, and answering irresistible sicknesses.

   Worldwide collaboration in worldwide wellbeing includes sharing data, assets, and ability to reinforce medical care frameworks and address wellbeing disparities. Cooperative endeavors reach out to antibody conveyance, pandemic readiness, and exploration on arising sicknesses. Discretionary drives are fundamental for arranging evenhanded admittance to immunizations, working with innovation move, and encouraging worldwide associations in medical care innovative work.

3. **Atomic Restraint and Arms Control:**
The counteraction of the multiplication of atomic weapons and the advancement of arms control address basic spaces where global collaboration is basic. Deals like the Arrangement on the Restraint of Atomic Weapons (NPT) exemplify discretionary endeavors to forestall the spread of atomic weapons and advance demilitarization. Confirmation components, strategic discoursed, and arms decrease arrangements add to worldwide endeavors to improve security and forestall the disastrous outcomes of atomic fighting.
In spite of strategic accomplishments in arms control, challenges continue in the demilitarization plan. Modernization of atomic arms stockpiles by certain states and the rise of new international elements highlight the requirement for continuous discretionary drives. Arrangements, for example, the Exhaustive Atomic Test-Boycott Deal (CTBT) and the Settlement on the Preclusion of Atomic Weapons (TPNW) address political undertakings to support standards against atomic weapons and advance the objective of an atomic liberated world.

4. **Financial Participation and Exchange Tact:**

Financial participation and exchange tact are necessary parts of global relations, encouraging monetary development and soundness. Economic alliance haggled through discretionary channels plan to work with the development of labor and products, make structures for settling debates, and advance financial coordination. Global associations like the World Exchange Association (WTO) give stages to discretionary talks and the goal of exchange related issues.

Monetary participation stretches out past exchange to include improvement help, obligation alleviation, and manageable advancement drives. Discretionary endeavors in this domain include arranging help bundles, cultivating monetary associations, and tending to variations in worldwide financial administration. In any case, monetary participation faces difficulties connected with exchange awkward nature, protectionism, and the lopsided dissemination of financial advantages, requiring continuous conciliatory endeavors to resolve these issues.

Difficulties and Potential open doors in Global Collaboration:
While worldwide participation is instrumental in tending to worldwide difficulties, it faces a few difficulties that request conciliatory artfulness and creative arrangements.

1. **Patriotism and Disintegration of Multilateralism:**
The ascent of patriotism in certain nations has prompted a retreat from multilateralism, testing the viability of global participation. The prioritization of public interests over aggregate activity can subvert political endeavors to address shared difficulties. Cases of nations pulling out from peaceful accords or establishments

signal a shift away from cooperative methodologies, presenting difficulties to the soul of collaboration.

To address this test, political drives ought to zero in on reaffirming the advantages of multilateralism and delineating how helpful endeavors can all the more likely location complex worldwide issues. Building agreement around the possibility that countries are more grounded together than alone is vital for encouraging a recharged obligation to multilateral participation.

2. **International Strains and Power Elements:**

International strains and power elements among significant states can obstruct successful tact. Contending interests, authentic complaints, and vital competitions make obstructions to discretionary goals of contentions and worldwide difficulties. Ambassadors frequently wrestle with exploring complex international scenes where public interests might outweigh helpful undertakings.

Strategic endeavors to address international pressures require building extensions of understanding and trust among countries. Certainty building measures, Track II discretion (casual discoursed), and intercession cycles can add to de-heightening contentions and making strategic openings for cooperative arrangements. Vital exchange and shared regard for every country's sway are fundamental components in beating power awkward nature.

3. **Absence of Implementation Systems:**

While peaceful accords and settlements are fundamental conciliatory devices, their viability relies upon the presence of strong requirement systems. Now and again, the shortfall of solid authorization systems restricts the capacity to consider states responsible for infringement. Strategic endeavors to resolve issues like denials of basic liberties or natural debasement might experience difficulties when states see negligible ramifications for rebelliousness.

Improving the enforceability of peaceful accords requires political endeavors to reinforce foundations liable for checking and consistence. States should surrender a level of power to aggregate systems that guarantee adherence to shared standards. Strategic drives zeroed in on supporting law and order at the worldwide level can add to the improvement of compelling requirement systems.

4. **Imbalance and Worldwide Differences:**

Worldwide imbalances in monetary turn of events, admittance to assets, and mechanical capacities present difficulties to global participation. Emerging nations might confront hardships in completely taking part in political exchanges or executing worldwide drives because of asset limitations and primary variations. Connecting these holes requires conciliatory endeavors to address underlying drivers and advance comprehensive collaboration.

Conciliatory drives pointed toward lessening worldwide imbalances ought to focus on improvement help, innovation move, and limit working in agricultural countries. Upholding for fair exchange rehearses, obligation help, and interests in schooling and medical services can add to making a more level battleground for countries with shifting degrees of monetary turn of events. A pledge to comprehensive discretion guarantees that the voices, everything being equal, no matter what their monetary standing, are heard and regarded.

5. **Network protection Dangers and Data Fighting:**
The computerized age has acquainted new difficulties with strategy, especially in the domains of network protection and data fighting. Negotiators should fight with the weaponization of data, cyberattacks, and the utilization of innovation to sabotage conciliatory endeavors. Building standards and arrangements to administer the internet is a continuous conciliatory test, requiring aggregate activity to address arising dangers to worldwide security.
Conciliatory endeavors in the domain of network protection include making peaceful accords that lay out rules of conduct in the internet. Standards against state-supported cyberattacks, standards of capable direct in the internet, and systems for attribution and responsibility are basic parts of conciliatory drives in this space. Empowering open exchange and collaboration among countries can add to the improvement of a protected and stable computerized climate.

6. **Environment of Question and Conciliatory Breakdowns:**

In certain examples, an environment of question among countries can prompt conciliatory breakdowns. Arguments about domain, authentic complaints, or political belief systems might prevent viable correspondence and joint effort. Modifying trust and encouraging open political channels become fundamental essentials for settling clashes and progressing shared objectives.

Discretionary endeavors to conquer doubt require a promise to discourse, straightforwardness, and compromise components. Track I and Track II strategy, certainty building measures, and intervention cycles can add to facilitating strains and setting out open doors for productive commitment. Developing a culture of discretion that focuses on discourse and struggle counteraction is fundamental for cultivating an additional helpful and interconnected world.

Chapter 8

The Role of Technology in Human Rights

The convergence of innovation and basic liberties is a perplexing and diverse domain that has developed fundamentally throughout the long term. As innovation keeps on progressing at an exceptional speed, its effect on common liberties turns out to be progressively articulated. This multifaceted connection among innovation and basic liberties incorporates a large number of perspectives, including reconnaissance, security, opportunity of articulation, admittance to data, and the right to a fair preliminary.

One of the most conspicuous regions where innovation and common freedoms meet is in the domain of reconnaissance. State run administrations and different substances are utilizing trend setting innovations, like facial acknowledgment, biometric information assortment, and mass reconnaissance frameworks, to screen people on a remarkable scale. While these innovations can be instrumental in keeping up with public wellbeing and security, they likewise represent a huge danger to protection and individual flexibilities.

Facial acknowledgment innovation, for instance, has turned into a pervasive device in different areas, including policing, control, and, surprisingly, business applications. Its capacity to distinguish people in view of facial elements raises worries about the disintegration of secrecy and the potential for misuse. In tyrant systems, this innovation is frequently utilized to smother contradiction and track the developments of political activists, prompting a chilling impact on free articulation.

Biometric information assortment goes past facial acknowledgment and incorporates the utilization of fingerprints, iris sweeps, and DNA profiling. While these advances can be significant for criminal examinations and boundary security, the mass assortment and capacity of biometric information raise worries about the gamble of abuse, wholesale fraud, and ridiculous interruptions into people's confidential lives. Finding some kind of harmony between security goals and the security of common freedoms stays a basic test in the computerized age.

Reconnaissance innovations are not restricted to actual spaces; they additionally stretch out into the advanced domain. States and partnerships participate in mass information assortment and checking of online exercises, presenting critical difficulties to one side to security. The disclosures by informants like Edward Snowden have uncovered the degree of worldwide observation programs directed by knowledge organizations, starting a worldwide discussion on the harmony between public safety and individual protection.

The appearance of the web and computerized correspondence advances has changed how data is scattered, got to, and controlled. While the web gives a stage to free articulation and the trading of thoughts, it likewise presents difficulties to conventional ideas of restriction and control. Legislatures all over the planet utilize different strategies, including content sifting, site hindering, and online observation, to manage the progression of data and smother contradict.

The idea of internet fairness is fundamental to guaranteeing equivalent and unhindered admittance to online substance. Nonetheless, the shortfall of internet fairness can prompt unfair practices, where certain substance or administrations are focused on over others. This not just influences the guideline of a level battleground yet in addition has suggestions for opportunity of articulation and admittance to data.

Web-based entertainment stages, with their tremendous client bases and impact, have become huge players in molding public talk. While these stages offer a space for people to put themselves out there and associate with others, they likewise face examination for their part in enhancing disinformation, disdain discourse, and online provocation. The spread of phony news and the control of online accounts present difficulties to one side to precisely get and bestow data.

State run administrations have additionally involved web-based entertainment for reconnaissance and oversight purposes. During seasons of political agitation, specialists might cinch down on web access, block virtual entertainment stages, or screen online exercises to smother difference and control the story. These activities encroach upon the right to opportunity of articulation and block the capacity of people to coordinate and activate for social or political causes.

The ascent of man-made reasoning (simulated intelligence) acquaints another aspect with the convergence of innovation and basic liberties. Computer based intelligence frameworks, fueled by AI calculations, can possibly reform different areas, from medical services to law enforcement. In any case, the sending of simulated intelligence likewise raises moral worries, especially with regards to dynamic cycles that influence people's lives.

Algorithmic predisposition is a major problem in the turn of events and execution of simulated intelligence frameworks. On the off chance that the information used to prepare these frameworks is one-sided, the calculations can sustain and try and fuel existing imbalances and segregation. For instance, artificial intelligence utilized in law enforcement frameworks might show racial or orientation predisposition, prompting treacherous results. Tending to algorithmic predisposition requires cautious thought of information assortment rehearses, straightforwardness in algorithmic navigation, and continuous assessment to alleviate potentially negative side-effects.

The utilization of artificial intelligence in policing muddles the connection among innovation and basic freedoms. Prescient policing, facial acknowledgment, and mechanized reconnaissance frameworks raise worries about the potential for prejudicial focusing on, encroachment on the assumption of honesty, and the disintegration of fair treatment privileges. Finding some kind of harmony between using innovation to upgrade policing and shielding individual privileges is a sensitive test that requires complete lawful systems and moral rules.

The right to a fair preliminary is a major common freedom that is progressively impacted by mechanical headways. The utilization of computerized proof, for example, messages, virtual entertainment posts, and electronic observation information, has become ordinary in judicial procedures. While these advances can improve the proficiency of examinations, they likewise bring up issues about the validness, unwavering quality, and suitability of computerized proof. Guaranteeing that overall sets of laws adjust to the developing idea of innovation while maintaining the standards of a fair preliminary is pivotal in keeping up with the trustworthiness of the equity framework.

The worldwide scene of common liberties is interconnected, and gives in a single region of the planet can have gradually expanding influences across borders. Innovation assumes a critical part in molding the elements of worldwide relations and impacting the advancement and security of common freedoms on a worldwide scale.

Computerized strategy, digital fighting, and the utilization of innovation in struggle zones are regions where the effect of innovation on basic liberties rises above public limits.

Computerized discretion, enveloping the utilization of innovation in global relations, has turned into a noticeable component of present day statecraft. State run administrations influence web-based entertainment, online stages, and computerized correspondence channels to draw in with worldwide crowds, advance their plans, and shape worldwide accounts. While computerized strategy can improve straightforwardness and work with diverse comprehension, it likewise raises worries about the potential for deception, promulgation, and the control of general assessment on a worldwide scale.

Digital fighting, including the utilization of advanced devices and methods to direct hostile activities in the virtual area, has critical ramifications for basic freedoms. Digital assaults on basic foundation, government frameworks, and confidential undertakings can upset fundamental administrations, compromise protection, and encroach on the right to security. The attribution of digital assaults and the advancement of standards and guidelines in the internet are continuous difficulties that require global collaboration and discourse.

In struggle zones, innovation is both a device of strengthening and a wellspring of weakness for people and networks. The utilization of online entertainment and computerized correspondence in struggle circumstances considers the scattering of data, assembly of assets, and coordination of aid ventures. Be that as it may, it likewise opens populaces to reconnaissance, control, and the gamble of designated assaults. The moral utilization of innovation in struggle zones, adherence to worldwide helpful regulation, and the assurance of weak populaces are basic contemplations in the developing scene of present day clashes.

The job of innovation in progressing monetary, social, and social freedoms is a blade that cuts both ways. On one hand, mechanical developments can possibly further develop admittance to schooling, medical services, and monetary open doors, especially in underserved and underestimated networks. Then again, the computerized partition, inconsistent admittance to innovation, and the grouping of force in the possession of a couple of innovation goliaths add to broadening social imbalances.

The right to instruction is personally associated with the open doors and difficulties introduced by innovation. Advanced learning stages, online assets, and instructive advancements can possibly democratize admittance to schooling and extension holes in learning potential open doors. Nonetheless, the advanced separation, described by differences in admittance to innovation and the web, compounds existing imbalances. Guaranteeing comprehensive and impartial admittance to advanced training is urgent for understanding the right to instruction for all.

Also, the right to wellbeing is impacted by mechanical headways in medical care conveyance, telemedicine, and advanced wellbeing records. Innovation can possibly further develop medical services results, increment productivity, and improve preventive measures. Notwithstanding, worries about information protection, the security of wellbeing data, and the potential for prejudicial practices in medical services calculations should be addressed to shield the right to wellbeing for all people.

The monetary effect of innovation on the option to work and fair work rehearses is a focal worry in the computerized age. Robotization, computerized reasoning, and advanced stages have changed the idea of work, prompting shifts in business designs and the gig economy. While innovation can set out new monetary open doors, it likewise raises worries about work removal, problematic working circumstances, and the disintegration of laborers' privileges. Laying out a structure that guarantees the security of laborers' freedoms even with mechanical progressions is fundamental for an equitable and comprehensive economy.

The grouping of force in the possession of innovation organizations and the rise of computerized syndications present difficulties to one side to partake in social life and partake in the advantages of logical advancement. The control of data, calculations, and online stages by a couple of substances raises worries about oversight, control, and the potential for the prohibition of different voices. Adjusting the requirement for development and financial development with the security of social variety and individual freedoms is an intricate undertaking that requires cautious thought of administrative structures and moral guidelines.

In the domain of protected innovation freedoms, innovation has changed how imaginative works are created, appropriated, and consumed. The digitization of content, web based real time features, and the expansion of client produced content present the two amazing open doors and difficulties for makers, shoppers, and the assurance of social legacy. Finding some kind of harmony between cultivating development and guaranteeing fair pay for makers while regarding the public's on the right track to get to data and culture is a continuous test in the advanced time.

The appearance of blockchain innovation presents additional opportunities for getting and safeguarding common liberties, especially in regions like personality the executives, monetary consideration, and straightforward administration. Blockchain's decentralized and alter safe nature can possibly upgrade the security of advanced personalities, work with monetary exchanges without customary mediators, and advance straightforwardness in government processes. Notwithstanding, the reception of blockchain additionally raises worries about protection, versatility, and the potential for unseen side-effects that might affect weak populaces.

As innovation keeps on propelling, the job of man-made brainpower, computerization, and mechanical technology in the labor force turns out to be progressively critical. While these advancements hold the commitment of expanded effectiveness, efficiency, and development, they likewise raise worries about work removal, monetary imbalance, and the requirement for reskilling and upskilling in the labor force. Finding some kind of harmony between embracing mechanical headways and guaranteeing that the advantages are shared impartially across society is a focal test in forming the future universe of work.

The connection among innovation and common liberties reaches out to the field of natural manageability. Environmental change, deforestation, contamination, and other natural difficulties are exacerbated by human exercises, a considerable lot of which include the utilization of innovation. Simultaneously, innovation can likewise assume a urgent part in relieving the effect of human exercises on the climate and advancing maintainable practices.

The right to a solid climate is characteristically connected to how innovation is tackled for practical turn of events. Sustainable power advances, savvy city drives, and creative answers for squander the executives are instances of how innovation can add to natural preservation. Notwithstanding, the ecological impression of innovation, including the creation and removal of electronic gadgets, should be painstakingly figured out how to forestall further mischief to biological systems and human wellbeing.

The digitalization of data and correspondence has suggestions for the option to get to data, a principal part of a straightforward and responsible society. While innovation has worked with the fast spread of data, it has additionally brought about difficulties, for example, data over-burden, falsehood, and the control of public talk. The option to get to precise and fair data is urgent for informed direction, urban commitment, and the working of vote based social orders.

The security of common liberties in the computerized age requires vigorous legitimate systems, moral guidelines, and global participation. Public and global regulations should adjust to the advancing scene of innovation to guarantee the security of individual privileges. Security regulations, information security guidelines, and regulations overseeing the utilization of observation advancements are basic parts of a lawful structure that shields common liberties in the computerized time.

Moral contemplations in the turn of events and arrangement of innovation are fundamental to forestall hurt and guarantee that mechanical progressions line up with basic freedoms standards. Moral rules for the utilization of man-made reasoning, biometric information, and reconnaissance advances assist with moderating the gamble of misuse and segregation. Drawing in technologists, policymakers, and common society in moral conversations is fundamental to encourage a mindful and human-driven way to deal with innovation.

Worldwide collaboration is pivotal in tending to the worldwide difficulties presented by the crossing point of innovation and basic liberties. The transnational idea of advanced innovations requires cooperative endeavors to lay out standards, guidelines, and norms that maintain basic liberties standards. Drives, for example, the Unified Countries' Core values on Business and Basic freedoms give a structure to organizations to regard common liberties in their tasks, including the utilization of innovation.

Common society assumes a critical part in pushing for basic freedoms in the computerized age. Non-administrative associations, activists, and backing bunches add to bringing issues to light, observing basic freedoms infringement, and considering states and partnerships responsible for their activities. The dynamic support of common society guarantees that assorted viewpoints are viewed as in forming strategies and practices that influence basic liberties.

Schooling and advanced proficiency are fundamental parts of engaging people to explore the computerized scene and exercise their freedoms. Advancing attention to online protection, computerized security, and capable advanced citizenship upgrades people's capacity to safeguard themselves and supporter for their privileges in the computerized circle. Instructive foundations, states, and common society associations assume a pivotal part in cultivating computerized education at different degrees of society.

All in all, the job of innovation in common liberties is complex and dynamic, enveloping a great many issues that touch upon the center standards of individual opportunities, correspondence, and nobility. As innovation keeps on propelling, the difficulties and open doors gave by its crossing point basic liberties will advance. Finding some kind of harmony between bridling the advantages of innovation for human advancement and defending the essential freedoms of people requires progressing exchange, coordinated effort, and a pledge to moral and comprehensive practices. decisions today will shape the eventual fate of a reality where innovation and basic liberties are entwined in manners that request cautious thought and mindful stewardship.

8.1 Exploration of the impact of technology on human rights

The effect of innovation on basic freedoms is a diverse investigation that digs into the perplexing manners by which progressions in innovation shape, challenge, and reclassify crucial parts of common liberties. As the computerized period unfurls, innovation turns into a basic piece of day to day existence, affecting everything from correspondence and data admittance to reconnaissance and individual security. This investigation expects to analyze the diverse elements of the connection among innovation and basic liberties, inspecting regions like protection, opportunity of articulation, observation, the right to a fair preliminary, and the more extensive ramifications on a worldwide scale.

Protection, a foundation of individual opportunity, faces remarkable difficulties in the computerized age. The unavoidable utilization of innovation, from cell phones to brilliant home gadgets, brings about the steady age and assortment of individual information. Virtual entertainment stages, web indexes, and different internet based benefits frequently track clients' exercises, inclinations, and areas, making broad advanced profiles. This mass collection of information raises worries about the potential for protection encroachment, observation, and the double-dealing of individual data for business or political purposes.

The universality of reconnaissance advances enhances these worries. States, policing, and confidential substances progressively utilize modern observation apparatuses like facial acknowledgment, biometric information assortment, and mass reconnaissance frameworks. While these advances might improve safety efforts, they likewise infringe upon people's protection privileges. Facial acknowledgment, for example, empowers the recognizable proof and following of people out in the open spaces, bringing up issues about the option to move unreservedly without steady observing.

Biometric information, incorporating fingerprints, iris sweeps, and DNA profiling, adds one more layer of intricacy to the security talk. While these advancements offer extraordinary identifiers for security purposes, their mass assortment and capacity present dangers of unapproved access, fraud, and possible abuse. Finding some kind of harmony between the security goals driving mechanical progressions and the assurance of individual protection stays a basic test in the developing scene of common liberties.

The right to opportunity of demeanor, a foundation of popularity based social orders, faces the two open doors and difficulties in the computerized domain. The web gives a stage to people overall to offer their viewpoints, thoughts, and sentiments. Virtual entertainment stages intensify voices, associate networks, and work with the trading of data. Notwithstanding, this freshly discovered computerized space likewise turns into a landmark where issues like internet based provocation, disdain discourse, and the spread of deception come to the front.

State run administrations and tyrant systems influence innovation to screen, control, and edit online substance, stifling contradiction and restricting opportunity of articulation. Web closures, content separating, and designated oversight encroach upon people's privileges to uninhibitedly access and scatter data. Finding some kind of harmony between fighting internet based hurts and maintaining the standards of free articulation requires nuanced approaches that regard common liberties and majority rule values.

The peculiarity of unhindered internet assumes a crucial part in guaranteeing equivalent and unlimited admittance to online substance. The shortfall of unhindered internet can prompt oppressive practices where certain substance or administrations get particular treatment, compromising the level battleground on the web.

Saving unhindered internet is fundamental for maintaining the rule that all data, no matter what its source, ought to be similarly available to clients, shielding the popularity based nature of the web.

Virtual entertainment stages, with their tremendous client bases and compelling calculations, contribute essentially to molding public talk. While these stages offer spaces for exchange, activism, and local area building, they additionally wrestle with difficulties connected with the spread of disinformation, protected, closed off environments, and algorithmic inclination. Finding some kind of harmony between encouraging solid web-based networks and moderating the unfortunate results of unrestrained computerized impact is a perplexing errand that includes moral contemplations, administrative structures, and continuous discourse.

Man-made consciousness (simulated intelligence) acquaints another aspect with the convergence of innovation and basic freedoms. AI calculations, controlling simulated intelligence frameworks, can possibly alter different areas, from medical services and law enforcement to training and money. Nonetheless, the arrangement of simulated intelligence additionally raises moral worries, especially in dynamic cycles that influence people's lives.

Algorithmic predisposition represents a critical test in the turn of events and execution of artificial intelligence frameworks. Assuming the information used to prepare these frameworks is one-sided, the calculations can propagate and try and worsen existing imbalances and segregation. For instance, man-made intelligence utilized in law enforcement frameworks might display racial or orientation predisposition, prompting out of line results. Tending to algorithmic predisposition requires cautious thought of information assortment rehearses, straightforwardness in dynamic cycles, and continuous assessment to relieve unseen side-effects.

The utilization of simulated intelligence in policing confuses the connection among innovation and basic liberties. Prescient policing, facial acknowledgment, and robotized observation frameworks raise worries about unfair focusing on, the encroachment on the assumption of guiltlessness, and the disintegration of fair treatment freedoms. Adjusting the usage of innovation to improve policing with defending individual privileges is a sensitive test that requires extensive legitimate systems and moral rules.

The right to a fair preliminary, an essential common liberty, is progressively impacted by innovative headways. The utilization of computerized proof, for example, messages, virtual entertainment posts, and electronic reconnaissance information, has become typical in judicial actions. While these innovations upgrade the proficiency of examinations, they additionally bring up issues about the genuineness, unwavering quality, and acceptability of advanced proof. Guaranteeing that overall sets of laws adjust to the developing idea of innovation while maintaining the standards of a fair preliminary is essential for keeping up with the honesty of the equity framework.

The worldwide scene of basic freedoms is interconnected, and gives in a single region of the planet can have expanding influences across borders. Innovation assumes a critical part in forming the elements of worldwide relations and impacting the advancement and security of common freedoms on a worldwide scale. Advanced discretion, digital fighting, and the utilization of innovation in struggle zones are regions where the effect of innovation on common freedoms rises above public limits.

Computerized strategy, enveloping the utilization of innovation in worldwide relations, has turned into an unmistakable element of present day statecraft. State run administrations influence virtual entertainment, online stages, and advanced correspondence channels to draw in with worldwide crowds, advance their plans, and shape worldwide accounts. While computerized strategy can upgrade straightforwardness and work with diverse comprehension, it likewise raises worries about the potential for falsehood, promulgation, and the control of general assessment on a worldwide scale.

Digital fighting, including the utilization of advanced devices and methods to direct hostile activities in the virtual space, has critical ramifications for basic freedoms. Digital assaults on basic foundation, government frameworks, and confidential ventures can disturb fundamental administrations, compromise protection, and encroach on the right to security. The attribution of digital assaults and the advancement of standards and guidelines in the internet are progressing difficulties that require worldwide participation and exchange.

In struggle zones, innovation is both a device of strengthening and a wellspring of weakness for people and networks. The utilization of online entertainment and computerized correspondence in struggle circumstances considers the spread of data, assembly of assets, and coordination of aid projects. Be that as it may, it likewise opens populaces to observation, control, and the gamble of designated assaults. The moral utilization of innovation in struggle zones, adherence to global philanthropic regulation, and the assurance of weak populaces are basic contemplations in the developing scene of present day clashes.

The financial, social, and social freedoms of people are likewise significantly affected by innovation. On one hand, mechanical developments can possibly further develop admittance to schooling, medical services, and financial open doors, especially in underserved and minimized networks. Then again, the computerized partition, inconsistent admittance to innovation, and the convergence of force in the possession of a couple of innovation monsters add to broadening social imbalances.

The right to schooling is personally associated with the open doors and difficulties introduced by innovation. Advanced learning stages, online assets, and instructive advancements can possibly democratize admittance to schooling and scaffold holes in learning open doors.

In any case, the advanced separation, portrayed by abberations in admittance to innovation and the web, worsens existing imbalances. Guaranteeing comprehensive and fair admittance to advanced instruction is critical for understanding the right to schooling for all.

Likewise, the right to wellbeing is affected by mechanical headways in medical services conveyance, telemedicine, and advanced wellbeing records. Innovation can possibly further develop medical services results, increment proficiency, and improve preventive measures. Be that as it may, worries about information protection, the security of wellbeing data, and the potential for unfair practices in medical care calculations should be addressed to shield the right to wellbeing for all people.

The monetary effect of innovation on the option to work and fair work rehearses is a focal worry in the computerized age. Computerization, man-made brainpower, and advanced stages have changed the idea of work, prompting shifts in business designs and the gig economy. While innovation can set out new monetary open doors, it likewise raises worries about work uprooting, unstable working circumstances, and the disintegration of laborers' privileges. Laying out a system that guarantees the security of laborers' freedoms notwithstanding innovative progressions is fundamental for an equitable and comprehensive economy.

The centralization of force in the possession of innovation organizations and the rise of advanced imposing business models present difficulties to one side to take part in social life and partake in the advantages of logical advancement. The control of data, calculations, and online stages by a couple of elements raises worries about restriction, control, and the potential for the prohibition of different voices. Adjusting the requirement for development and financial development with the security of social variety and individual privileges is a mind boggling task that requires cautious thought of administrative systems and moral principles.

In the domain of protected innovation freedoms, innovation has changed how imaginative works are delivered, dispersed, and consumed. The digitization of content, internet web-based features, and the multiplication of client produced content present the two amazing open doors and difficulties for makers, shoppers, and the assurance of social legacy. Finding some kind of harmony between cultivating development and guaranteeing fair remuneration for makers while regarding the public's all in all correct to get to data and culture is a continuous test in the computerized time.

The appearance of blockchain innovation presents additional opportunities for getting and safeguarding basic liberties, especially in regions like personality the executives, monetary consideration, and straightforward administration. Blockchain's decentralized and alter safe nature can possibly upgrade the security of computerized characters, work with monetary exchanges without customary middle people, and advance straightforwardness in government processes.

Nonetheless, the reception of blockchain additionally raises worries about protection, adaptability, and the potential for unseen side-effects that might affect weak populaces.

As innovation keeps on propelling, the job of man-made brainpower, robotization, and advanced mechanics in the labor force turns out to be progressively critical. While these advancements hold the commitment of expanded effectiveness, efficiency, and development, they likewise raise worries about work removal, monetary disparity, and the requirement for reskilling and upskilling in the labor force. Finding some kind of harmony between embracing mechanical headways and guaranteeing that the advantages are shared fairly across society is a focal test in forming the future universe of work.

The connection among innovation and basic liberties reaches out to the field of ecological supportability. Environmental change, deforestation, contamination, and other ecological difficulties are exacerbated by human exercises, a considerable lot of which include the utilization of innovation. Simultaneously, innovation can likewise assume an essential part in moderating the effect of human exercises on the climate and advancing supportable practices.

The right to a solid climate is inherently connected to how innovation is outfit for maintainable turn of events. Sustainable power advances, shrewd city drives, and imaginative answers for squander the executives are instances of how innovation can add to ecological preservation. In any case, the ecological impression of innovation, including the creation and removal of electronic gadgets, should be painstakingly figured out how to forestall further damage to environments and human wellbeing.

The digitalization of data and correspondence has suggestions for the option to get to data, a principal part of a straightforward and responsible society. While innovation has worked with the fast spread of data, it has likewise led to difficulties, for example, data over-burden, deception, and the control of public talk. The option to get to precise and fair data is significant for informed direction, community commitment, and the working of popularity based social orders.

The assurance of common liberties in the computerized age requires powerful lawful systems, moral principles, and global participation. Public and worldwide regulations should adjust to the advancing scene of innovation to guarantee the assurance of individual privileges. Security regulations, information insurance guidelines, and regulations overseeing the utilization of reconnaissance innovations are basic parts of a lawful system that shields common freedoms in the computerized time.

Moral contemplations in the turn of events and sending of innovation are fundamental to forestall hurt and guarantee that mechanical headways line up with common freedoms standards.

Moral rules for the utilization of man-made reasoning, biometric information, and observation advancements assist with moderating the gamble of misuse and separation. Connecting with technologists, policymakers, and common society in moral conversations is fundamental to encourage a dependable and human-driven way to deal with innovation.

Worldwide collaboration is pivotal in tending to the worldwide difficulties presented by the convergence of innovation and common liberties. The transnational idea of advanced innovations requires cooperative endeavors to lay out standards, guidelines, and norms that maintain basic liberties standards. Drives, for example, the Unified Countries' Core values on Business and Basic liberties give a structure to organizations to regard common freedoms in their tasks, including the utilization of innovation.

Common society assumes a urgent part in supporting for basic liberties in the computerized age. Non-administrative associations, activists, and promotion bunches add to bringing issues to light, observing common freedoms infringement, and considering states and partnerships responsible for their activities. The dynamic support of common society guarantees that different points of view are viewed as in molding strategies and practices that influence basic freedoms.

Schooling and computerized proficiency are fundamental parts of enabling people to explore the advanced scene and exercise their freedoms. Advancing attention to online protection, computerized security, and capable computerized citizenship improves people's capacity to safeguard themselves and backer for their freedoms in the computerized circle. Instructive foundations, states, and common society associations assume a urgent part in cultivating computerized education at different degrees of society.

8.2 Opportunities and challenges presented by advancements in AI, surveillance, and communication

Headways in man-made brainpower (simulated intelligence), reconnaissance innovations, and correspondence frameworks present a range of chances and difficulties that shape the direction of society in significant ways. As we explore the intricacies of the computerized age, it becomes basic to fundamentally look at the complex effect of these innovative progressions on different features of our lives, going from protection and security to the financial scene. This investigation dives into the amazing open doors and difficulties emerging from the tireless walk of progress in man-made intelligence, observation, and correspondence advances.

Man-made intelligence, with its capacity to reproduce shrewd way of behaving, has arisen as an extraordinary power across different areas. The valuable open doors introduced by simulated intelligence are tremendous, promising expanded productivity, advancement, and the capacity to handle complex issues. In medical services, artificial intelligence applications can upgrade analytic exactness, customize therapy designs, and assist drug disclosure. The potential for computer based intelligence to reform medical care conveyance and further develop patient results is an encouraging sign for the fate of clinical science.

Also, in the domain of training, simulated intelligence can possibly customize opportunities for growth, adjust to individual understudy needs, and give significant experiences to teachers. Shrewd mentoring frameworks, versatile learning stages, and man-made intelligence driven instructive substance can take care of different learning styles, encouraging a more comprehensive and viable instructive climate. The democratization of information through artificial intelligence driven schooling apparatuses can possibly address variations in admittance to quality training around the world.

The business scene is additionally going through critical changes powered by man-made intelligence. Mechanization and AI calculations smooth out processes, enhance asset allotment, and add to information driven navigation. From production network the board to client relationship the executives, computer based intelligence fueled arrangements upgrade hierarchical effectiveness, empowering organizations to remain cutthroat in an undeniably powerful and complex worldwide market.

Notwithstanding, close by these potential open doors, man-made intelligence presents a large group of difficulties that require cautious thought. One such test is the moral utilization of man-made intelligence, particularly concerning predisposition in calculations. Assuming that man-made intelligence frameworks are prepared on one-sided datasets, they can sustain and try and fuel existing imbalances. For instance, one-sided simulated intelligence calculations in employing cycles may unexpectedly victimize specific socioeconomics, supporting fundamental predispositions. Tending to these moral worries requires straightforward and capable man-made intelligence improvement works on, progressing investigation, and a promise to decency and value.

Reconnaissance innovations have likewise seen critical headways, bringing up significant issues about the harmony between security objectives and individual protection privileges. The valuable open doors introduced by observation advancements in improving public security are clear. Facial acknowledgment, biometric information assortment, and prescient examination can help policing in forestalling and settling wrongdoings. Observation frameworks out in the open spaces can go about as an obstruction to crimes, adding to the general security of networks.

Nonetheless, the extension of reconnaissance capacities likewise presents difficulties to security freedoms. Mass observation, whether led by states or confidential elements, can bring about the steady checking of people's exercises. The assortment and capacity of huge measures of individual information raise worries about expected misuse, unapproved access, and the disintegration of protection. Finding some kind of harmony between guaranteeing public security and shielding individual protection requires hearty lawful structures, straightforwardness, and systems for responsibility.

The utilization of observation advances stretches out past actual spaces into the computerized domain. States and partnerships participate in mass information assortment and observing of online exercises, provoking the right to protection in the period of advanced correspondence. The disclosures by informants about worldwide reconnaissance programs have touched off banters about the limits between public safety interests and individual security privileges. Safeguarding advanced security requires thorough information assurance guidelines, encryption norms, and a continuous exchange about the constraints of reconnaissance in the computerized period.

Correspondence advancements, driven by the quick development of the web, have reformed how data is dispersed, got to, and controlled. The valuable open doors introduced by prompt worldwide correspondence are monstrous. Web-based entertainment stages, online discussions, and computerized specialized devices empower people to interface, share thoughts, and sort out on a scale beforehand inconceivable. The democratization of data enables individuals to partake in broad daylight talk, challenge severe systems, and activate for social and political causes.

Notwithstanding, similar correspondence advancements likewise present difficulties to the respectability of data and the option to get to exact and fair satisfied. The spread of falsehood, counterfeit news, and online promulgation can have extensive outcomes on popular assessment, political cycles, and social attachment. Calculations intended to amplify client commitment might add to the making of online closed quarters, supporting existing convictions and polarizing public talk. Tending to these difficulties requires a multi-layered approach including media proficiency schooling, algorithmic straightforwardness, and mindful substance control rehearses.

The coming of web-based entertainment, while giving a stage to different voices, has likewise led to worries about web-based badgering, disdain discourse, and the abuse of individual information. The obscurity managed the cost of by online stages can encourage people to take part in hurtful ways of behaving, establishing a computerized climate where the line between free articulation and online maltreatment becomes obscured. Safeguarding the right to opportunity of articulation in the computerized age requires the improvement of viable balance components, lawful systems that address online badgering, and a promise to making comprehensive web-based spaces.

The amazing open doors and difficulties introduced by computer based intelligence, observation, and correspondence advancements are interconnected and add to the developing scene of common freedoms. The joining of these advances brings up issues about the fate of work, monetary imbalance, and the convergence of force in the possession of a couple. Mechanization and artificial intelligence driven developments in the work environment can possibly build efficiency and effectiveness yet in addition raise worries about work dislodging and the effect on laborers' privileges.

The gig economy, worked with by computerized stages, acquaints new difficulties with conventional work systems. Laborers in the gig economy frequently face problematic working circumstances, need employer stability, and might be avoided from customary work securities. Adjusting the adaptability and open doors gave by the gig economy the need to guarantee fair work practices and social insurances is a mind boggling task that requires imaginative strategy arrangements.

The grouping of force in the possession of innovation organizations and the rise of advanced syndications additionally present difficulties to contest, purchaser privileges, and the more extensive financial scene. A couple of tech monsters control tremendous measures of client information, shape online stories, and impact market elements. Controlling the force of these substances while cultivating development and rivalry is a fragile difficult exercise that requires worldwide collaboration and ground breaking strategy systems.

The convergence of computer based intelligence, reconnaissance, and correspondence innovations additionally has worldwide ramifications for common freedoms. Computerized discretion, digital fighting, and the utilization of innovation in struggle zones are regions where the effect of innovation rises above public limits. Computerized discretion use innovation in worldwide relations, empowering legislatures to draw in with worldwide crowds, shape accounts, and lead statecraft in the advanced domain. Nonetheless, worries about disinformation, digital assaults, and the weaponization of innovation in international contentions highlight the requirement for worldwide standards and guidelines in the internet.

Digital fighting, including the utilization of computerized apparatuses for hostile activities in the virtual area, acquaints new difficulties with the right to security and the assurance of basic foundation. The attribution of digital assaults, the improvement of standards in the internet, and worldwide participation in tending to digital dangers are basic parts of a worldwide reaction to the developing scene of computerized struggle.

In struggle zones, innovation becomes both a device of strengthening and a wellspring of weakness. The utilization of virtual entertainment and computerized correspondence takes into consideration the dispersal of data, activation of assets, and coordination of aid ventures. Notwithstanding, it likewise opens populaces to reconnaissance, control, and the gamble of designated assaults. Guaranteeing the moral utilization of innovation in struggle zones, adherence to global compassionate regulation, and the assurance of weak populaces are basic contemplations in the advancing scene of current contentions.

As society wrestles with the valuable open doors and difficulties introduced by computer based intelligence, reconnaissance, and correspondence innovations, it becomes obvious that an extensive and comprehensive methodology is important. Moral contemplations, legitimate structures, and worldwide participation are vital in exploring the intricacies of the advanced age.

Finding some kind of harmony between saddling the advantages of innovative headways and defending central common liberties requires progressing exchange, interdisciplinary cooperation, and a guarantee to moral and comprehensive practices.

8.3 Cybersecurity and protecting digital rights

In the consistently developing scene of the computerized age, the advantageous connection among network safety and the security of advanced privileges becomes the overwhelming focus. As innovation keeps on propelling, the dependence on computerized stages, online correspondence, and interconnected frameworks develops dramatically. With this expanded network comes the basic to get advanced frameworks and shield the major privileges of people in the computerized domain. This investigation dives into the mind boggling transaction between network safety measures and the security of computerized freedoms, tending to the difficulties, valuable open doors, and moral contemplations inborn in this unique relationship.

Network safety as a Mainstay of Computerized Freedoms Security

At its center, network protection includes the execution of measures to safeguard PC frameworks, organizations, and advanced information from unapproved access, assaults, and harm. As people, organizations, and states progressively depend on advanced advances for correspondence, business, and basic framework, the significance of hearty network safety rehearses becomes principal in maintaining computerized freedoms.

Security and Information Assurance: One of the major computerized freedoms is the right to protection. Network safety estimates assume a vital part in defending individual data from unapproved access and information breaks. Encryption advancements, secure validation conventions, and severe access controls add to the assurance of delicate information, guaranteeing that people have command over their own data in the computerized space.

Opportunity of Articulation: In the computerized domain, opportunity of articulation is worked with through different web-based stages and correspondence channels. Network safety estimates that guard against oversight, online observation, and digital assaults pointed toward smothering free discourse are fundamental for safeguarding this computerized right. The assurance of informants, writers, and activists from advanced dangers empowers the free progression of data and different points of view.

Admittance to Data: The option to get to data is a foundation of popularity based social orders. Online protection shields, like secure organizations and versatile data frameworks, add to guaranteeing continuous admittance to data. Safeguarding against digital assaults that intend to control or confine admittance to data is basic for maintaining the computerized right to information.

Security of Individual Gadgets: With the multiplication of individual gadgets associated with the web, getting these gadgets against digital dangers becomes vital to safeguarding computerized freedoms. Cell phones, PCs, and shrewd contraptions frequently store delicate individual data, and network safety measures, for example, gadget encryption and secure confirmation systems assist with forestalling unapproved access and safeguard clients' advanced personalities.

Difficulties to Network safety and Advanced Privileges

While network safety measures are fundamental for safeguarding computerized freedoms, they face a bunch of difficulties in the consistently developing scene of the internet. Ill-disposed entertainers, developing assault vectors, and the quick speed of mechanical change present intricacies that request steady variation and advancement in the domain of online protection.

Digital Danger Scene: The idea of digital dangers is dynamic and multi-layered. Malignant entertainers, going from individual programmers to state-supported elements, utilize refined strategies, for example, phishing, malware, ransomware, and refusal of-administration assaults to think twice about frameworks. The continually developing danger scene requires online protection experts to remain in front of arising dangers and weaknesses.

Computerized Disparity: The worldwide advanced partition acquaints difficulties with network safety and computerized privileges. Differences in admittance to innovation and computerized proficiency can leave specific populaces more helpless against digital dangers. Connecting the advanced gap and elevating comprehensive admittance to computerized assets are fundamental stages in guaranteeing that network protection estimates benefit all people, regardless of financial status or geographic area.

Observation and Protection Worries: While network safety measures are intended to safeguard against unapproved access, there is a fragile harmony between security goals and individual protection freedoms. Government reconnaissance programs, mass information assortment, and the utilization of observation advancements can infringe upon the right to security. Finding some kind of harmony between guaranteeing public safety and defending individual protection is a continuous test in the advanced age.

Moral Ramifications of Network safety Practices: The moral contemplations encompassing online protection rehearses come to the bleeding edge as innovations like computerized reasoning and AI are progressively incorporated into security frameworks. Inquiries concerning algorithmic predisposition, prejudicial profiling, and the moral utilization of digital abilities highlight the requirement for straightforward and responsible network safety rehearses that line up with common liberties standards.

Open doors for Improving Online protection and Advanced Freedoms

In exploring the difficulties presented by the dynamic digital scene, there are open doors for cooperative energies between network safety measures and the security of advanced freedoms. Proactive techniques, global collaboration, and a promise to moral network safety practices can add to a safer and freedoms regarding computerized climate.

Multistakeholder Coordinated effort: Tending to the diverse difficulties of network protection and advanced privileges requires cooperation among state run administrations, confidential area elements, common society, and the specialized local area. A multistakeholder approach empowers different points of view, skill, and assets to be offered of real value, cultivating extensive arrangements that balance security and privileges contemplations.

Worldwide Standards and Participation: Network protection is intrinsically a worldwide issue, and global collaboration is urgent in tending to transnational digital dangers. Laying out global standards, arrangements, and systems for mindful state conduct in the internet can add to a more steady and secure computerized climate. The advancement of instruments for sharing danger knowledge and organizing reactions upgrades aggregate network safety endeavors.

Limit Building and Computerized Education: Enabling people with computerized proficiency abilities and encouraging mindfulness about network protection best practices add to a stronger computerized society. Instructive projects, preparing drives, and limit building endeavors help clients perceive and moderate digital dangers, lessening the probability of succumbing to digital assaults and improving in general network protection.

Mechanical Developments: Persistent innovative progressions give open doors to creative network safety arrangements. Computerized reasoning and AI advancements can be utilized to recognize and answer digital dangers continuously. Secure-by-plan standards, where network safety is incorporated into the advancement of computerized frameworks all along, add to building stronger and intrinsically secure innovations.

Security Improving Advancements: The turn of events and reception of protection upgrading innovations (PETs) offer arrangements that accommodate network safety with protection freedoms. Methods like differential security, homomorphic encryption, and decentralized character frameworks add to safeguarding individual information while as yet considering viable network safety measures. Coordinating PETs into online protection systems mitigates security concerns.

Moral Contemplations in Network safety

As the field of network safety develops, moral contemplations become progressively significant in guaranteeing that the security of computerized freedoms is led in a way predictable with more extensive moral standards. A few key moral contemplations merit consideration in the domain of online protection.

Client Assent and Independence: Regarding client assent and independence is a basic moral rule. Network protection measures ought to be carried out with straightforwardness, and clients ought to have the organization to arrive at informed conclusions about the assortment, use, and capacity of their advanced information. Clear and reasonable terms of administration, assent systems, and easy to understand interfaces add to moral online protection rehearses.

Proportionality and Need: Network protection measures ought to be corresponding to the dangers they mean to address and ought to just gather and use information that is essential for their expected purposes. Keeping away from unreasonable information assortment and guaranteeing that network protection measures don't excessively encroach on individual security freedoms are key moral contemplations in the plan and execution of network safety procedures.

Non-Separation and Inclusivity: Network safety practices ought to be planned and carried out without segregation, guaranteeing that they don't lopsidedly influence specific gatherings in light of elements like race, orientation, or financial status. Inclusivity in network safety configuration implies considering the requirements and points of view of assorted client gatherings to forestall unexpected predispositions and segregation.

Responsibility and Straightforwardness: Moral network safety rehearses request responsibility and straightforwardness from both public and confidential area elements. Obviously imparting online protection arrangements, practices, and episodes to impacted parties constructs trust and permits people to consider associations responsible for their activities. Straightforwardness about the extension and limits of network protection estimates oversees assumptions and cultivates a culture of responsibility.

Basic liberties Effect Evaluations: Leading common freedoms influence evaluations (HRIAs) is a proactive moral measure in network protection. Evaluating the expected effect of network safety rehearses on common liberties permits associations to recognize and alleviate any antagonistic impacts on people's privileges. Coordinating HRIAs into the turn of events and sending of network protection measures guarantees a human-driven approach.

Looking Forward: Adjusting Security and Freedoms

As the computerized scene keeps on advancing, finding the sensitive harmony between network safety objectives and the insurance of advanced freedoms stays a continuous test. The convergence of innovative progressions, legitimate structures, and moral contemplations will shape the future direction of network safety rehearses and their effect on individual privileges.

Legitimate Structures for Network protection: Public and global lawful systems assume a urgent part in laying out the boundaries for online protection rehearses. Regulation tending to information security, protection privileges, and network safety obligations gives an establishment to moral and freedoms regarding online protection measures. Constant updates and transformations of lawful systems to address arising difficulties are fundamental.

Moral Rules and Norms: Creating and complying to moral rules and principles in online protection is urgent for guaranteeing mindful lead. Proficient associations, industry affiliations, and network safety professionals ought to team up to lay out and advance moral standards that focus on the assurance of basic liberties. Moral contemplations ought to be incorporated into network safety preparing and confirmation programs.

Public Talk and Informed Navigation: Connecting with general society in talk about the compromises among network protection and computerized privileges cultivates informed direction. Open discourse about the moral contemplations innate in online protection rehearses helps fabricate a mutual perspective of the difficulties and valuable open doors, permitting society to on the whole decide the OK furthest reaches of network safety measures.

Mechanical Advancement and Transformation: Embracing mechanical development and adjusting network protection practices to advancing dangers are fundamental for remaining in front of digital enemies. Notwithstanding, this development should be directed by moral contemplations, guaranteeing that innovative progressions line up with common liberties standards. A culture of persistent improvement and versatility is fundamental in the steadily changing scene of network protection.

Worldwide Participation: Online protection is a worldwide test that requires worldwide arrangements. Global participation, data sharing, and cooperative endeavors among states, confidential area substances, and common society are fundamental for tending to cross-line digital dangers. Creating shared standards and rules that focus on common freedoms in the internet adds to a safer and privileges regarding computerized biological system.

Chapter 9

Ensuring a Lasting Legacy

Guaranteeing an enduring heritage is a pursuit that rises above individual lives, venturing into the texture of social orders and societies. An immortal undertaking tries to make history, an imprint that endures the erosive powers of time. Whether on an individual level or inside the more extensive setting of foundations and civic establishments, the idea of an enduring heritage sparkles consideration about the idea of effect, importance, and the getting through impression of human life.

At its center, the craving to leave an enduring heritage is profoundly imbued in the human mind. From antiquated human advancements to the current day, people and networks have looked to be recalled, to have their commitments recognized, and to impact the course of history. The journey for an enduring heritage is complex, entwining with ideas of personality, reason, and the fleetingness of life. As mortal creatures, people wrestle with the temporariness of their reality, provoking a characteristic tendency to make something that outlives their restricted time on The planet.

One of the principal roads through which people intend to guarantee an enduring heritage is through their achievements and commitments to their main subject areas. In the domains of science, writing, craftsmanship, and different disciplines, trailblazers endeavor to push the limits of information, abandoning a collection of work that mirrors their scholarly ability as well as impacts resulting ages. Logical disclosures, artistic magnum opuses, and notable works of art act as demonstrations of the human limit with regards to creation and the getting through force of thoughts.

Consider the transcending figures of history whose inheritances persevere through their scholarly commitments. Consider Aristotle, whose philosophical works keep on molding the manner in which we ponder morals, transcendentalism, and governmental issues. Ponder the persevering through effect of Leonardo da Vinci, whose creative brightness and logical interest made a permanent imprint on the Renaissance and then some. These figures epitomize the limit of people to rise above their human limits by diverting their energies into pursuits that rise above the quick setting of their lives.

However, the quest for an enduring inheritance isn't bound to the domains of scholarly and imaginative undertakings. People likewise look to abandon a heritage through their activities, values, and the effect they have on the existences of others. Thoughtful gestures, mentorship, and generosity are roads through which people can shape the world in a manner that stretches out past their fleeting presence. The so-called far reaching influence of positive activities can resound through ages, making a tradition of sympathy, compassion, and social improvement.

In the contemporary scene, givers like Bill and Melinda Doors represent the potential for utilizing abundance and impact to resolve squeezing worldwide issues. Through their establishment, they have committed significant assets to drives pointed toward further developing medical care, schooling, and decreasing neediness. Their heritage isn't just monetary; it is woven into the texture of the lives they contact and the extraordinary effect of their altruistic endeavors.

Essentially, pioneers who champion civil rights, balance, and common liberties try to abandon a heritage that rises above their time in office. Figures like Nelson Mandela, who battled against politically-sanctioned racial segregation in South Africa, and Martin Luther Ruler Jr., a conspicuous figure in the American social equality development, are recalled for their initiative as well as for the significant cultural changes they motivated. Their heritages persevere as images of flexibility, boldness, and the continuous battle for equity.

The mission for an enduring inheritance isn't exclusively a singular undertaking; it stretches out to the shared perspective of networks and civilizations. Organizations, both strict and mainstream, try to implant their qualities and convictions in the chronicles of history. The development of great designs, the protection of social practices, and the engendering of aggregate stories all add to the perseverance of a social inheritance that traverses ages.

Consider the antiquated developments that raised building wonders like the Pyramids of Giza, the Incomparable Mass of China, and the Acropolis. These designs were not simply accomplishments of designing; they were statements of social character, indications of the aggregate yearnings and convictions of social orders that tried to carve their reality into the woven artwork of mankind's set of experiences. The perseverance of these designs addresses the force of aggregate undertakings in forming the tradition of civilizations.

Strict establishments, as well, assume an essential part in forming the social and moral tradition of social orders. The sacred texts, customs, and lessons went down through ages act as an ethical compass, directing followers and giving a feeling of coherence across time. The getting through impact of strict texts, like the Good book, the Quran, or the Bhagavad Gita, features the job of otherworldliness in forming the qualities that support human advancements.

In any case, the mission for an enduring heritage isn't without its intricacies and inconsistencies. The actual idea of heritage infers a craving for recognition, affirmation, and an enduring effect. In this pursuit, people and establishments wrestle with inquiries of self image, lowliness, and the moral ramifications of their activities. The pressure between private desire and a veritable longing to add to everyone's benefit highlights the ethical issues intrinsic in the mission for an enduring heritage.

Think about the polarity between sacrificial assistance and self-glorification. Demonstrations of charity, for example, can be certifiable articulations of philanthropy, driven by a longing to ease enduring and add to the benefit of everyone. In any case, they can likewise be damaged by the longing for public acknowledgment, making a sensitive harmony between the quest for a positive effect and the self image driven need for praise. The test lies in exploring this offset with respectability, guaranteeing that the thought process behind activities is established in a veritable obligation to having an effect.

Besides, the actual idea of heritage is emotional and dependent upon the viewpoints of the people who acquire it. What one individual or society considers as a positive and persevering through inheritance might be seen diversely by others. This subjectivity presents a component of flightiness and highlights the intricacy of making a heritage that resounds across different social, social, and verifiable settings.

In the domain of legislative issues, pioneers wrestle with the test of offsetting quick strategy objectives with the drawn out prosperity of their countries. The choices they make, whether in the domain of monetary arrangement, natural stewardship, or worldwide relations, have suggestions that reach out a long ways past their time in office. The tradition of political pioneers is many times molded by the outcomes of their decisions, whether those results manifest in monetary success, social solidness, or the safeguarding of popularity based values.

The mission for an enduring heritage likewise converges with the human tendency to rise above mortality through the production of persevering through images and stories. Landmarks, sculptures, and dedicatory ceremonies act as unmistakable articulations of the human craving to be recalled. Be that as it may, these images are not safe to the progression of time, and their implications can develop as cultural qualities shift.

Consider the contentions encompassing landmarks that celebrate verifiable figures with complex inheritances. Sculptures of people who were once celebrated as legends might turn into the point of convergence of discussions about equity, value, and verifiable responsibility. The reconsideration of such images mirrors the unique idea of aggregate memory and the continuous exchange about which parts of history ought to be praised and which ought to be basically analyzed.

The computerized age has acquainted new aspects with the journey for an enduring inheritance. In a time of extraordinary network, people can shape their computerized personas, abandoning a path of information that frames a virtual impression. Virtual entertainment stages, web journals, and online discussions offer people the open door to organize and disperse parts of their lives, adding to the development of a computerized heritage that reaches out past actual presence.

Nonetheless, the computerized domain brings its own arrangement of difficulties and moral contemplations. The lastingness of computerized data brings up issues about protection, assent, and the potential for post mortem control of one's web-based presence. The advanced heritage, while offering uncommon open doors for self-articulation, additionally highlights the requirement for people to practice watchfulness and purposefulness in molding their web-based personalities.

The getting through nature of an inheritance is complicatedly connected to the idea of impact — the capacity to profoundly mold the considerations, ways of behaving, and desires of others. Pioneers, whether in the domains of legislative issues, business, or culture, use impact that can either add to the improvement of society or sustain unsafe belief systems. The obligation that accompanies impact highlights the ethical basic to utilize power wisely and morally.

Think about the impact of social symbols in forming cultural standards and values. Performers, entertainers, and specialists, through their inventive articulations, can impact general assessment, challenge cultural standards, and add to social movements. Be that as it may, this impact isn't absent any trace of moral contemplations. Craftsmen, similar to some other wielders of impact, wrestle with inquiries of obligation, responsibility, and the possible effect of their work on different crowds.

The idea of an enduring heritage reaches out past the individual and cultural levels to the worldwide field. Mankind faces squeezing difficulties that request aggregate activity and a common obligation to guaranteeing the prosperity of people in the future. Issues, for example, environmental change, natural corruption, and worldwide imbalance highlight the interconnectedness of human life and the basic to think about the drawn out results of present-day choices.

Notwithstanding these difficulties, the quest for an enduring heritage takes on a more extensive importance — a guarantee to stewardship, manageability, and the protection of the planet for people in the future. Pioneers in government, business, and common society are called upon to rise above transient interests and embrace an all encompassing methodology that focuses on the drawn out wellbeing of the planet. The tradition of our age will be characterized, to a limited extent, by the moves we initiate to address these worldwide difficulties and the effect of those activities on the direction of human civilization.

The mission for an enduring heritage is innately attached to the human experience of time. The consciousness of mortality, the short lived nature of life, and the craving for congruity brief people to examine the imprint they will leave on the world. This examination isn't grim; rather, it is an affirmation of the limited idea of human life and the significant chance to add to something that rises above the singular self.

As people and social orders wrestle with the intricacies of inheritance, it becomes clear that the pursuit is certainly not a singular excursion yet an aggregate undertaking that traverses ages. Guardians look to leave an inheritance for their kids, giving qualities, insight, and a feeling of personality. Teachers try to significantly influence the personalities of future pioneers, furnishing them with the information and abilities to explore the difficulties of their time. Every age acquires the traditions of those that go before it and, thusly, adds to the continuous story of mankind's set of experiences.

In this aggregate pursuit, the job of schooling arises as a key part in forming a heritage that perseveres. Instructive foundations, from grade schools to colleges, act as pots for the transmission of information, the development of decisive reasoning, and the supporting of values that support an equitable and economical society. The tradition of schooling reaches out past the homeroom, affecting the directions of people and social orders as they explore the intricacies of the advanced world.

Besides, the journey for an enduring inheritance welcomes contemplation about the idea of progress and satisfaction. In a world frequently determined by measurements of material riches, distinction, and outside approval, people are tested to observe the genuine importance of an everyday routine very much experienced. The quest for a significant inheritance requires a nuanced comprehension of progress — one that rises above shallow markers and embraces an all encompassing vision of prosperity.

The entwining of individual and aggregate heritages highlights the intergenerational idea of the human experience. Guardians plant seeds of shrewdness and values that prove to be fruitful in the existences of their kids. Pioneers and thought pioneers plant the seeds of thoughts that sprout and bloom in the personalities of people in the future. The aggregate tradition of mankind is an embroidery woven by incalculable people across time, each contributing a string to the complex story of human advancement.

As people ponder their own inheritances, they are faced with the basic to adjust their activities to their qualities and desires. The quest for an enduring inheritance is definitely not a uninvolved undertaking; it requires deliberateness, trustworthiness, and a promise to settling on decisions that impact one's feeling of direction. This arrangement among values and activities is the quintessence of genuineness — a quality that rises above time and leaves a persevering through engrave on the world.

Chasing an enduring heritage, people are stood up to with the dualities innate in the human experience — the strain between the vaporous and the everlasting, the individual and the group, the material and the profound. An excursion requests a fragile harmony among aspiration and modesty, between the craving for acknowledgment and the obligation to caring help. In this fragile dance, people explore the intricacies of the human condition, looking to make a story that rises above the limits of individual lives.

9.1 Strategies for preserving and advancing the legacy of human rights

Safeguarding and propelling the tradition of common liberties is a basic errand that requires a complex and supported exertion on neighborhood, public, and worldwide levels. Common freedoms, including the innate pride and uniformity, all things considered, structure the bedrock of just and empathetic social orders. Be that as it may, regardless of impressive advancement in the acknowledgment and security of common liberties, challenges continue, requiring smart procedures to maintain and broaden these key standards.

At the core of any system for safeguarding and propelling the tradition of basic liberties is the acknowledgment that common freedoms are general, indissoluble, and unavoidable. This implies that each person, paying little mind to identity, nationality, orientation, or some other trademark, is qualified for similar essential privileges and opportunities. To guarantee the persevering through pertinence of basic liberties, endeavors should be coordinated towards encouraging a worldwide culture that perceives and regards this all inclusiveness.

Training arises as a strong device in such manner. By integrating basic freedoms training into school educational programs, social orders can impart a comprehension of the standards, history, and meaning of common liberties since the beginning.

This instructive methodology not just outfits people with the information to declare their privileges yet additionally develops an aggregate ethos that qualities and safeguards the respect of all citizenry. The objective is to engage people to become advocates for basic freedoms inside their networks and then some.

Also, propelling the tradition of basic liberties requires facing verifiable treacheries and recognizing the effect of fundamental separation. Truth and compromise processes, as exemplified by drives in post-politically-sanctioned racial segregation South Africa or post-massacre Rwanda, give roads to social orders to deal with their past and manufacture a way towards mending. By recognizing verifiable wrongs and looking for change, networks can lay the basis for an additional fair and comprehensive future.

In the domain of worldwide relations, the advancement of basic freedoms requires strategic endeavors that rise above public limits. Countries should take part in open discourse, sharing prescribed procedures and tending to deficiencies in their separate basic liberties records. Global settlements and arrangements, like the General Statement of Common freedoms and the Worldwide Contract on Common and Political Privileges, give systems to participation and responsibility. States should approve these arrangements as well as effectively carry out and implement the specified basic liberties principles.

Couple with political endeavors, the job of non-administrative associations (NGOs) and common society is vital. These elements act as guard dogs, considering legislatures responsible for denials of basic freedoms and upholding for positive change. NGOs frequently work on the cutting edges, offering help to underestimated networks, reporting basic freedoms infringement, and intensifying the voices of the individuals who may some way or another go unheard. Engaging and safeguarding crafted by these associations is indispensable to the more extensive methodology for propelling the tradition of common liberties.

Lawful systems, both public and global, assume a urgent part in safeguarding and propelling basic freedoms. Strong legitimate systems, including established securities and exhaustive regulation, act as the establishment for guaranteeing that basic liberties are optimistic goals as well as enforceable principles. Successful legitimate foundations, including free legal authorities and unprejudiced policing, are fundamental for considering culprits of common liberties infringement responsible.

The foundation and reinforcing of worldwide courts, like the Global Lawbreaker Court (ICC), add to the worldwide battle against exemption. These foundations assume a basic part in arraigning people liable for terrible denials of basic liberties, indicating to the worldwide local area that there will be ramifications for such activities. Be that as it may, the viability of these systems relies upon the collaboration of countries and their obligation to maintaining law and order.

Notwithstanding lawful components, the media assumes a significant part in molding public discernments and impacting strategy. A free and free media fills in as a guard dog, uncovering denials of basic liberties, uncovering debasement, and encouraging public mindfulness. Columnists and news sources that work unafraid of retaliation add to the spread of data that can assemble popular assessment and strain legislatures to regard common liberties.

However, the media's true capacity for positive effect is dependent upon its obligation to unprejudiced announcing and keeping away from emotionalism. Dependable news coverage is necessary to cultivating an educated public that can effectively participate in conversations encompassing basic freedoms issues. Media proficiency projects can additionally upgrade the public's capacity to basically assess data, recognize realities from deception, and add to a more educated and connected with populace.

Moreover, orientation correspondence is an essential component of any system for safeguarding and propelling common liberties. Ladies and young ladies keep on confronting foundational segregation and savagery around the world. Endeavors to address orientation based segregation and savagery should be thorough, including lawful changes, instructive drives, and social intercessions. Enabling ladies monetarily, socially, and politically isn't just a question of equity yet in addition an essential basic for making social orders that regard and safeguard the freedoms, everything being equal.

Comprehensive administration is one more key part of propelling basic freedoms. Legislatures should effectively include underestimated networks in dynamic cycles, guaranteeing that strategies and regulations mirror the different necessities and points of view of the populace. Inclusivity stretches out to minority gatherings, native networks, and other generally underestimated populaces. Laying out components for significant cooperation in administration assists with redressing verifiable treacheries and fabricate a more evenhanded and just society.

Monetary equity is indivisible from basic freedoms. Neediness, disparity, and financial double-dealing are ramifications of basic freedoms infringement as well as underlying drivers. A system for propelling common freedoms should incorporate measures to address financial incongruities and guarantee that all people approach essential necessities like food, medical care, training, and noble work. Social security nets, moderate tax collection, and arrangements that elevate monetary inclusivity add to the acknowledgment of financial privileges.

Innovation, while offering extraordinary open doors for availability and data sharing, additionally presents difficulties to basic freedoms. The advanced age has seen the ascent of reconnaissance innovations, online restriction, and dangers to security. Saving and propelling common liberties in the computerized period requires a cautious adjusting of the advantages of mechanical progressions with the security of individual opportunities. Legitimate systems, moral rules, and worldwide participation are fundamental in tending to the moral and basic freedoms ramifications of arising advances.

Besides, encouraging a culture of compassion and fortitude is major to the safeguarding and headway of common freedoms. A general public that values sympathy is bound to dismiss separation, prejudice, and narrow mindedness. Instructive projects and drives that advance social trade and understanding add to the development of a worldwide local area that perceives the common humankind, everything being equal. Compassion fills in as a strong remedy to the dehumanization that frequently goes before denials of basic liberties.

In struggle zones and regions impacted by compassionate emergencies, the assurance of basic liberties is frequently seriously compromised. Furnished clashes can prompt mass removal, inescapable brutality, and a breakdown of law and order. Protecting and propelling common liberties in such settings requires deliberate global endeavors, including peacekeeping missions, compassionate guide, and strategic drives pointed toward settling the basic reasons for struggle.

Global fortitude is essential in supporting countries wrestling with the result of contention or cataclysmic events. Giving help to impacted networks, modifying foundation, and supporting the foundation of responsible administration structures add to the rebuilding of basic freedoms in post-struggle settings. Temporary equity components, including truth and compromise commissions, assume an imperative part in tending to past outrages and encouraging a feeling of equity and conclusion.

All in all, safeguarding and propelling the tradition of common liberties requests a complete and cooperative methodology. Instructive drives, lawful systems, conciliatory endeavors, media commitment, and monetary approaches all assume necessary parts in maintaining basic freedoms standards. The interconnected idea of common freedoms requires techniques that address the main drivers of infringement and advance a culture of compassion, inclusivity, and equity.

While progress has been made in the worldwide acknowledgment of basic liberties, challenges endure. The acknowledgment of common liberties requires a continuous obligation to cautiousness, responsibility, and the quest for equity. In an undeniably interconnected world, where the activities of one country can have broad results, global collaboration is principal. The protection and headway of common freedoms are not simply moral objectives; they are fundamental for building a world that regards the intrinsic respect and worth of each and every person.

9.2 Education and awareness initiatives

Training and mindfulness drives stand as pivotal support points in cultivating positive cultural change, handling different issues, and engaging people to pursue informed choices. Whether tending to social treacheries, advancing natural supportability, or upholding for wellbeing and prosperity, these drives assume a critical part in molding aggregate mentalities and ways of behaving.

The effect of training and mindfulness resonates across different areas, adding to the improvement of informed residents, cultivating sympathy, and catalyzing developments for positive change.

One of the essential targets of schooling and mindfulness drives is to give information and develop decisive reasoning abilities. In the domain of formal training, schools and colleges act as key foundations for the transmission of information. Educational plan configuration, showing philosophies, and instructive assets all add to molding the scholarly scene of people. An educational plan that coordinates different viewpoints, addresses current cultural difficulties, and cultivates basic request furnishes understudies with the instruments to mindfully draw in with the world.

Past conventional instructive settings, casual and non-formal training drives likewise assume a huge part. Studios, workshops, and local area based programs give roads to learning outside the bounds of homerooms. These drives take care of different crowds, including grown-ups, minimized networks, and people with restricted admittance to formal schooling. By taking on a long lasting learning viewpoint, training and mindfulness drives can engage people to adjust to a quickly impacting world, ceaselessly update their abilities, and participate in continuous self-awareness.

Besides, schooling and mindfulness drives act as a strong method for tending to cultural disparities. Admittance to quality instruction has for quite some time been perceived as a critical determinant of social portability and financial open door. Endeavors to connect instructive holes, particularly for underestimated networks, are fundamental for destroying foundational hindrances. Grants, mentorship programs, and designated instructive mediations add to making a more comprehensive and fair instructive scene.

As well as cultivating scholarly development, training and mindfulness drives assume a critical part in creating social and the capacity to understand people on a deeper level. These drives add to the development of compassion, understanding, and a feeling of shared liability. By presenting people to different points of view and encounters, training turns into a device for building spans across cultural partitions. Drives that advance social trade, discourse, and inclusivity add to the improvement of socially cognizant and humane people.

Natural mindfulness and training are fundamental parts of endeavors to address the raising environmental difficulties confronting the planet. Drives in this area expect to advise people about the effect regarding human exercises on the climate, bring issues to light about environmental change, and advance feasible practices. Natural schooling, whether incorporated into formal educational plans or conveyed through local area programs, outfits people with the information and abilities to settle on biologically cognizant decisions.

Moreover, wellbeing training and mindfulness drives are instrumental in advancing individual and public prosperity. Illuminating people group about preventive medical services measures, solid ways of life, and the significance of emotional wellness adds to making better social orders. Programs that address marks of disgrace related with emotional well-being, substance misuse, or explicit ailments assume an essential part in cultivating a steady and informed local area.

The advanced age has fundamentally extended the scope and effect of training and mindfulness drives. Innovation empowered learning stages, online courses, and intelligent instructive assets have democratized admittance to data. These drives rise above geological limits, making instruction available to people around the world. Also, web-based entertainment and online stages act as useful assets for scattering data, encouraging exchange, and preparing aggregate activity.

While the advanced scene presents open doors, it additionally presents difficulties, including issues of falsehood and computerized partitions. Training and mindfulness drives should adjust to the advancing computerized setting, consolidating computerized proficiency parts to engage people to basically explore online spaces. Battling deception and advancing media proficiency are fundamental parts of guaranteeing that schooling in the computerized age is a power for positive change.

Training and mindfulness drives are fundamental to resolving social issues like separation, imbalance, and unfairness. Variety and incorporation preparing, against inclination training, and projects that challenge generalizations add to making more open minded and populist social orders. Drives that feature the chronicles and encounters of minimized networks assist with balancing verifiable eradications and encourage a more comprehensive comprehension of cultural stories.

Besides, with regards to common freedoms, schooling fills in as an integral asset for strengthening and backing. Common freedoms schooling drives expect to illuminate people about their privileges, advance comprehension of global basic liberties principles, and enable networks to advocate for equity and correspondence. By cultivating a culture of common liberties, these drives add to the counteraction of misuses, the strengthening of weak populaces, and the formation of an additional fair and impartial world.

In the domain of orientation balance, training and mindfulness drives are vital for destroying generalizations, testing prejudicial practices, and advancing orientation comprehensive conditions. Orientation delicate training educational plans, mindfulness crusades about orientation based savagery, and drives that empower the support of ladies in customarily male-ruled fields add to making more impartial social orders. Also, advancing attention to different orientation characters and articulations is a fundamental part of cultivating comprehensive and strong networks.

The crossing point of training and monetary strengthening is clear in drives that attention on expertise advancement, business venture, and monetary proficiency. Outfitting people with reasonable abilities, encouraging pioneering mentalities, and elevating monetary education add to financial flexibility and independence. These drives are especially significant for minimized networks and people confronting obstructions to monetary support.

Urban instruction is fundamental for sustaining dynamic and informed residents who can contribute seriously to majority rule processes. Drives that advance metro commitment, political education, and a comprehension of administration structures engage people to partake in forming their networks and considering pioneers responsible. By ingraining a feeling of community obligation, these drives add to the imperativeness of vote based social orders.

An all encompassing way to deal with schooling and mindfulness perceives the interconnectedness of different social issues. Drives that embrace an interconnected viewpoint, recognizing the covering aspects of personality and honor, add to a more nuanced comprehension of cultural difficulties. Multifaceted training cultivates sympathy, supports allyship, and prepares people to explore the intricacies of an inexorably different and interconnected world.

With regards to worldwide difficulties, like the Unified Countries Supportable Improvement Objectives (SDGs), schooling and mindfulness drives assume a focal part. The SDGs envelop a scope of interconnected goals, including destroying neediness, guaranteeing admittance to quality training, advancing orientation correspondence, and fighting environmental change. Training arises as a cross-cutting subject, filling in as an impetus for progress across different SDGs.

To augment the effect of schooling and mindfulness drives, joint effort and associations are fundamental. Joint effort between states, instructive establishments, non-benefit associations, and the confidential area upgrades the span and adequacy of drives. Public-private associations, specifically, can use assets, mastery, and advancement to address complex cultural difficulties.

Assessment and appraisal are basic parts of powerful training and mindfulness drives. Checking the effect of projects, gathering input, and adjusting methodologies in view of proof add to persistent improvement. Thorough assessment processes assist with recognizing fruitful methodologies, evaluate the necessities of interest groups, and refine drives to all the more likely address the developing difficulties of the networks they serve.

Be that as it may, challenges persevere in the execution of schooling and mindfulness drives. Asset requirements, especially in minimized networks and creating locales, present critical hindrances to the powerful conveyance of schooling programs.

Addressing these moves requires a guarantee to evenhanded asset dissemination, inventive financing models, and an emphasis on coming to underserved populaces.

Protection from change and profoundly imbued predispositions can likewise block the outcome of mindfulness drives. Drives that challenge existing standards, whether connected with orientation jobs, racial generalizations, or social practices, may confront resistance. Defeating obstruction requires a blend of key correspondence, local area commitment, and the development of neighborhood champions who can advocate for positive change.

9.3 Individual and collective responsibilities in upholding human rights

Individual and aggregate liabilities in maintaining common freedoms are key parts of making a fair and evenhanded society. Basic liberties, grounded in the standards of nobility, fairness, and equity, request the dynamic commitment of people and networks to guarantee their assurance and advancement. While states assume a pivotal part in laying out legitimate systems and foundations, the obligation to regard, secure, and satisfy common freedoms reaches out to each citizen. Perceiving and satisfying these obligations is fundamental for cultivating a culture of basic freedoms that rises above individual activities and adds to the prosperity of the worldwide local area.

At the singular level, a pledge to maintaining common freedoms starts with one's very own profound comprehension privileges and the privileges of others. Training and mindfulness drives assume a basic part in engaging people with the information and devices to perceive, state, and shield common liberties. This incorporates a comprehension of the Widespread Statement of Common liberties and other worldwide arrangements that lay out the essential privileges and opportunities to which each individual is entitled.

Besides, people should develop a feeling of compassion and a promise to treating others with pride and regard. Compassion is the underpinning of perceiving the mankind in others, paying little heed to contrasts in race, orientation, religion, or financial status. It includes recognizing the battles and difficulties looked by others and understanding that everybody has innate worth and privileges that should be maintained. Developing sympathy adds to the production of a more caring and comprehensive society where basic liberties are esteemed and safeguarded.

Individual obligation in maintaining common liberties likewise involves dynamic support in municipal life. This incorporates practicing the option to cast a ballot, participating in tranquil fights, and pushing for strategies that advance equity and equity. Being an educated and dynamic resident is a strong method for adding to the popularity based processes that shape the legitimate and strategy structures overseeing common liberties. Contribution in local area associations, basic liberties gatherings, and civil rights drives gives roads to people to have a significant effect in their nearby environmental factors.

Moreover, people should be watchful against separation and bias in their ordinary cooperations. Testing generalizations, predispositions, and unfair practices adds to cultivating a climate where everybody can reside liberated from separation. This includes shunning taking part in unfair way of behaving as well as effectively going up against and tending to separation when seen. By facing foul play at the singular level, people add to the more extensive development for common liberties.

At the aggregate level, networks, organizations, and social orders share an obligation to establish conditions that maintain common freedoms. This includes laying out lawful and strategy systems that safeguard the privileges, all things considered, guaranteeing equivalent admittance to open doors and assets, and effectively advancing inclusivity. Aggregate liability expects networks to go up against foundational issues like bigotry, sexism, and different types of segregation that propagate imbalance and foul play.

Organizations, including instructive, legislative, and corporate substances, assume a significant part in maintaining common liberties. Instructive foundations, specifically, have the obligation to establish comprehensive conditions that encourage a comprehension of variety and regard for basic freedoms. Educational program plan, strategies against segregation, and the advancement of decisive reasoning add to forming people who are mindful of their freedoms as well as focused on maintaining the privileges of others.

Legislatures bear a special obligation as obligation conveyors to regard, secure, and satisfy the basic freedoms of their residents. This includes making and implementing regulations that shield individual opportunities, guaranteeing admittance to fundamental administrations like medical care and training, and tending to social and monetary imbalances. Legislatures should likewise consider themselves responsible for basic freedoms infringement, giving instruments to change and equity when misuses happen.

Worldwide collaboration is fundamental for tending to worldwide basic liberties challenges. Countries should team up to resolve issues, for example, environmental change, displaced person emergencies, and the infringement of common liberties on a worldwide scale. Worldwide associations, including the Unified Countries, assume a significant part in setting worldwide guidelines, observing denials of basic freedoms, and organizing reactions to guarantee that common liberties are maintained generally.

Monetary organizations and companies likewise bear a huge obligation in maintaining basic freedoms. Past agreeing with work regulations, organizations should guarantee fair wages, safe working circumstances, and impartial open doors for all representatives. Corporate social obligation goes past benefit making to incorporate a pledge to moral strategic policies that regard and advance common freedoms. Also, organizations should be aware of their effect on neighborhood networks and the climate, perceiving that maintainable practices are entwined with common liberties contemplations.

Aggregate liability reaches out to the security of weak populaces, including exiles, travelers, and dislodged people. In the midst of contention or emergency, the global local area has an obligation to give helpful help and safeguard the privileges of those escaping oppression. Cooperative endeavors to address the underlying drivers of removal, advance harmony, and backing maintainable improvement add to the aggregate liability to around the world maintain common freedoms.

Media and correspondence stages likewise assume a crucial part in molding public discernments and impacting cultural perspectives towards basic liberties. Capable news-casting includes precise announcing, staying away from sentimentality, and testing deception. News sources should perceive the power they employ in forming general assessment and add to cultivating a culture that regards and values common liberties.

Common society associations, including non-administrative associations (NGOs), promotion gatherings, and grassroots developments, are fundamental in considering states and foundations responsible for basic liberties infringement. These associations frequently work on the cutting edges, archiving mishandles, offering help to impacted networks, and pushing for strategy changes. The aggregate endeavors of common society add to the balanced governance that shield basic liberties inside a general public.

In any case, aggregate liability requires more than responsive measures to address common freedoms infringement. It requests proactive endeavors to address the underlying drivers of fundamental issues. This includes testing designs of imbalance, destroying oppressive approaches, and effectively advancing social and financial equity. Aggregate liability expects social orders to defy verifiable shameful acts, recognizing the effect of past wrongs, and doing whatever it may take to correct them.

Besides, cultivating a culture of responsibility is basic to aggregate liability. This incorporates holding people, establishments, and state run administrations responsible for common freedoms infringement and it is guaranteed that equity. Laying out instruments for responsibility, including free oversight bodies, legal frameworks, and truth and compromise commissions, adds to making a culture where exemption isn't endured.

9.4 Looking towards the future: the ongoing evolution of human rights

The continuous development of common freedoms mirrors a dynamic and diverse excursion that answers the advancing difficulties and desires of humankind. Established in standards of nobility, fairness, and equity, basic freedoms have adjusted to the evolving socio-political scene, mechanical progressions, and a more profound comprehension of the interconnectedness of worldwide issues.

Looking towards the future, a few key aspects shape the continuous development of common freedoms, including the effect of arising innovations, the basic of ecological equity, the interconnection of privileges, and the proceeded with journey for inclusivity and uniformity.

Arising advancements, especially in the domain of computerized reasoning, biotechnology, and advanced observation, present the two open doors and difficulties to the fate of basic liberties. As innovation keeps on progressing at a remarkable speed, questions emerge about the moral ramifications and potential dangers related with these developments. The right to security, for instance, faces new dangers in a time of far and wide observation, information assortment, and the utilization of calculations that can encroach upon individual independence. Finding some kind of harmony between innovative advancement and the assurance of common freedoms requires strong legitimate structures, moral rules, and continuous discourse between technologists, policymakers, and basic liberties advocates.

Besides, the computerized age has changed the scene of opportunity of articulation and data. While the web gives a stage to different voices and the free progression of data, it likewise intensifies the spread of deception, online provocation, and control. The option to get to data faces new difficulties as legislatures and confidential elements try to control online spaces. Safeguarding the standards of opportunity of articulation in the computerized time expects endeavors to battle online control, safeguard computerized privileges, and guarantee that the web stays a device for strengthening as opposed to a wellspring of mistreatment.

With regards to arising innovations, the moral components of biotechnology and hereditary designing additionally raise basic common freedoms contemplations. The potential for headways in regions, for example, quality altering and man-made brainpower to affect the right to wellbeing, protection, and non-separation requires cautious moral reflection and worldwide joint effort. As science and innovation keep on pushing the limits of what is conceivable, the common liberties system should adjust to address novel difficulties and forestall the abuse of these advancements in manners that disregard key basic freedoms.

Natural equity arises as a focal subject in the continuous development of basic liberties, mirroring an expanded familiarity with the interconnectedness between human prosperity and the soundness of the planet. The right to a solid climate is progressively perceived as fundamental to the more extensive common liberties system. Environmental change, deforestation, contamination, and the exhaustion of normal assets present existential dangers to the acknowledgment of a noble and maintainable life for present and people in the future. Tending to natural difficulties requires a rights-based approach that thinks about the effect of ecological debasement on weak networks, recognizes the lopsided weight borne by minimized gatherings, and underscores the aggregate liability of countries to shield the planet.

The right to a sound climate crosses with other common liberties, like the right to life, wellbeing, and a sufficient way of life. Ecological corruption frequently fuels existing disparities and excessively influences minimized networks. Native people groups, for instance, every now and again endure the worst part of ecological obliteration as their territories are taken advantage of for asset extraction. Perceiving the connections between natural equity and basic freedoms is basic for building a feasible and impartial future.

Notwithstanding ecological equity, the continuous development of basic liberties stresses the interconnection of privileges — the acknowledgment that people might encounter numerous types of separation and that the insurance of freedoms should address the mind boggling exchange of different characters. Multifacetedness recognizes that elements like race, orientation, sexual direction, incapacity, and financial status meet to shape people's encounters of separation and honor.

The diversity focal point prompts a more nuanced comprehension of common freedoms, perceiving that specific gatherings might confront intensified types of separation and minimization. Endeavors to address foundational imbalances should consider the meeting characters that add to people's weaknesses. This approach is especially significant in regions, for example, enhancement in law enforcement, access, and instructive open doors, where people from minimized bunches frequently face layered types of separation.

Additionally, propelling common liberties with regards to interconnection requires a comprehensive and participatory methodology that focuses the voices and encounters of those generally impacted by separation. Networks should be effectively engaged with the plan and execution of approaches and drives pointed toward advancing common freedoms. Multifacetedness challenges the one-size-fits-all way to deal with common liberties promotion, encouraging an additional logical and comprehensive comprehension that mirrors the different real factors of people and networks.

The journey for inclusivity and balance stays a foundation of the continuous development of common liberties. While critical headway has been made in propelling the privileges of minimized gatherings, challenges endure, and the obligation to inclusivity should stay resolute. The privileges of ladies, LGBTQ+ people, racial and ethnic minorities, and people with handicaps keep on being regions where support and activism are fundamental for testing oppressive practices and destroying foundational hindrances.

Orientation balance, specifically, is a basic element of the continuous development of common liberties. The battle against orientation based brutality, segregation, and inconsistent open doors is interwoven with more extensive endeavors to internationally propel common liberties. Accomplishing orientation equity requires tending to male centric standards, enabling ladies and young ladies financially and socially, and testing fundamental boundaries that limit their full support in all circles of life.

The freedoms of LGBTQ+ people are additionally at the very front of the developing common liberties scene. Support for the decriminalization of homosexuality, the acknowledgment of same-sex connections, and the assurance of LGBTQ+ people from separation is a continuous worldwide exertion. The battle for LGBTQ+

privileges crosses with more extensive issues of human poise, opportunity of articulation, and the option to live liberated from viciousness and segregation.

Moreover, the continuous development of common freedoms requests a guarantee to handicap privileges and the full consideration of people with inabilities in all parts of society. This incorporates guaranteeing openness, sensible facilities, and testing cultural mentalities that sustain disgrace and separation. Perceiving the organization and independence of people with incapacities is crucial to the standards of common freedoms.

The privileges of outcasts and transients address one more basic aspect in the continuous development of common liberties. As the world wrestles with constrained dislodging, clashes, and philanthropic emergencies, safeguarding the privileges of those looking for shelter is a moral and lawful objective. This incorporates maintaining the option to look for refuge, guaranteeing sympathetic treatment, and tending to the underlying drivers of uprooting. The worldwide local area's reaction to the evacuee emergency highlights the interconnectedness of common freedoms and the requirement for global collaboration to address shared difficulties.

The continuous development of basic freedoms likewise requests a reconsideration of financial equity and the option to work. Monetary disparities, unsafe business, and the effect of computerization on the work market present difficulties to the acknowledgment of the option to work in honorable circumstances. Endeavors to address monetary abberations should consider the more extensive social and financial elements that add to disparity and focus on strategies that advance fair wages, laborers' freedoms, and comprehensive financial development.

With regards to medical care, the continuous development of common freedoms highlights the significance of guaranteeing widespread admittance to quality medical care administrations. The Coronavirus pandemic has featured the weaknesses inside medical care frameworks and the differences in admittance to clinical consideration. The right to wellbeing envelops the shortfall of sickness as well as the accessibility of fundamental medical care benefits, the social determinants of wellbeing, and the option to take part in choices influencing one's wellbeing.

The continuous advancement of common liberties requires an immovable obligation to responsibility and equity for basic freedoms infringement. Momentary equity systems, including truth and compromise commissions, assume a significant part in tending to verifiable treacheries and guaranteeing responsibility for denials of basic liberties. The quest for equity is fundamental for recuperating networks, forestalling the repeat of infringement, and maintaining the standards of basic liberties.

Worldwide basic liberties instruments, including the Global Crook Court (ICC), add to the worldwide battle against exemption for the most serious violations. The ICC's command to indict people for massacre, atrocities, and violations against humankind mirrors the global local area's obligation to considering culprits responsible.

In any case, the adequacy of these components relies upon the collaboration of states, the authorization of decisions.